The Multi-Hyphen Method

Also by Emma Gannon

Ctrl Alt Delete: How I Grew Up Online

The Multi-Hyphen Method

*Work less, create more, and design
a career that works for you*

Emma Gannon

**HODDER &
STOUGHTON**

First published in Great Britain in 2018 by Hodder & Stoughton
An Hachette UK company

3

Copyright © Emma Gannon 2018

A CIP catalogue record for this title is available from the British Library

Hardback ISBN 9781473680104
eBook ISBN 9781473680135

Typeset in Celeste by Hewer Text UK Ltd, Edinburgh
Printed and bound in Great Britain by Clays Ltd, Elcograf S.p.A.

Hodder & Stoughton policy is to use papers that are natural, renewable
and recyclable products and made from wood grown in sustainable
forests. The logging and manufacturing processes are expected to
conform to the environmental regulations of the country of origin.

Hodder & Stoughton Ltd
Carmelite House
50 Victoria Embankment
London EC4Y 0DZ

www.hodder.co.uk

Contents

Introduction

When it comes to your career, do you ever feel like you are on an endless journey to get somewhere and you never quite seem to arrive at the destination? This *somewhere* feels sort of like the top of a mountain: you can't quite see it, but if you squint, you think you can see something blurry and special in the distance waiting for you. When you eventually get there, tired and exhausted, you assume everything will magically fall into place. You will eventually achieve career nirvana. You were told somewhere along the way, maybe at school, that you'd reach this life goal in the end if you kept working hard and it's the reason you toil away at work, nine-to-five (and then some), every day. We will get that reward, someday. When we get another promotion, another pay rise, another perk to post on Instagram, it will surely get us further towards this place of calm and satisfaction. But what if such a place doesn't exist? What if, when you get there, there seems to be something missing? On the way up and during those long hours at work, have you ever truly thought about what success really looks like to you? The daily small successes, the mundane stuff, the choices you make along the way? What if the success you were promised at the top of the mountain were to not feel or look how you expected? What if success has an entirely different meaning to each of us and we might be currently risking totally missing the point? What a scam that would be.

There are things we have to do and unless you're extremely fortunate, work is one of them. But every single career guide I was given at school was outdated by the time I graduated. Even as recently as 2007, I was given the standard vet, teacher, lawyer multiple-choice brochure before I left university without any clue as to what was happening in the real world. In their defence, a realistic guide to working life can't possibly exist. For example, every single job I've had since graduating hadn't been invented when I was given these guides.

I also realise in hindsight that it wasn't only the act of *picking* a job that was frightening, it was the idea of *picking one job for life*. I was told and retold the myth that you can find your one dream path. I was encouraged to pick one subject to study, one subject to master. But successes in my career have come from having multiple projects, goals and choices. You don't have to pick one job or be good at one thing. In fact, the positives and possibilities of living a multi-hyphenate lifestyle are endless, hence this book. Some of us – most of us – are not built to dedicate our lives to just one thing.

The gig economy is on the rise. In the dictionary it's described as 'a labour market characterised by the prevalence of short-term contracts or freelance work as opposed to permanent jobs'. In America, it's predicted that by 2020 nearly half of all workers will earn some of their income from freelance projects. However, it also has a bit of a bad rap: last-minute scheduling, insecure hours, zero-hour contracts. The Multi-Hyphen Method is not championing these things, but it is taking into account that the gig-economy trend on the whole is on the rise. Being a multi-hyphenate is about choosing and strategising a plan of attack and having the freedom to take on multiple projects, not being backed into a corner. This is about choosing a lifestyle. This is about taking some power back into our own hands.

The multi-hyphenate lifestyle is about having a mishmash of projects going on with different income streams attached that make up a salary, instead of it coming from one source. Sure, it makes the 'What do you do?' question harder to answer, but your identity becomes less about what your singular job title is. It becomes more about who you are, what you are interested in, what pays the bills and what your hobbies are. All these things make up your different 'hyphens'. You are a career chameleon, changing and moulding yourself to different projects.

It's an important topic, work, as we spend so long doing it and even though it doesn't necessarily define who we are, it does make up a large proportion of what we do with our days.

On average we spend twelve years at work during our life-time and fifteen months of that will be time spent working late in addition to our contracted hours. And it will surprise no one to hear we now spend a third of our waking lives on our phones.[1] So, how do we thrive in a modern technology-obsessed work environment, cut through the noise, build longevity and create our own definitions of success? How do we make ourselves happier and more fulfilled in a world that wants us to chase a never-ending finish line? How do we launch that side-hustle that we keep talking about but feel like we don't know how to start? How do we stand out in a world where seven billion people are now joined in one interconnected online mass? How do we make money differently? How do we empower ourselves when we can feel so let down by an outdated system that doesn't work for so many? This book is my attempt to help you answer these questions.

The time frame needed for drastic change (in careers, lifestyle habits, technology) is faster than ever before. We don't have as much time to sit back and figure out a new plan of attack. Even if we do, we feel the anxiety and strain of the future upon us. We are all thinking about our career 2.0. We cannot predict the jobs we will do in the future, but we can keep ourselves feeling secure in a new way. The impact of technology is not all positive, but it's allowed us to teach ourselves new skills, create new jobs and build personal brands that over time attract consistent work.

The Multi-Hyphen Method is a practical look at how we can reinvent ourselves, the workplace, our environment and our own definition of personal success, with a toolkit in Chapter 7. It's about rethinking old habits and asking more questions. It's about designing our own schedules and not feeling limited to one thing or one box. In times of change, being really good at one thing isn't enough anymore.

THE MULTI-HYPHEN METHOD IS NOT:
- a guide to being a blogger/model/DJ – sorry
- a book just for generation slashie millennials
- celebrating the idea of insecure job-hopping
- a guide on how to be a freelancer
- a one-size-fits-all guidebook

THE MULTI-HYPHEN METHOD IS:

- a look at how we future-proof ourselves in the new world of work
- a reflection on the many ways we are being held back by workplace traditions of the past
- a toolkit on how to be many different things all at once
- a challenge to find new and personal definitions of success
- how to use technology to empower us in our future careers
- a new movement towards working less and creating more with your time

Technology has allowed us to rebel against what has been the norm for so many years. It has given us more freedom than we ever dreamed of. We can change our set parameters of the working day, use tools and machinery to tick off items on our work to-do list and communicate with others around the world with a click of a button. The Internet has led to rises and falls too, for example: the fall of large-scale glossy magazines and the rise of our own curated magazines by real people on Instagram; the fall of traditional celebrity and the rise of Internet fame of the everyday person. We have the opportunity to start a business in our bedrooms without traditional funding, just with Wi-Fi, some online crowdfunding and a good idea. Not everyone wants to be Mark Zuckerberg and conquer the world, but a lot of people want to give their idea a go, maybe even on the side of a job. Because we can. And with new industries also comes new gaps in the market. According to Emma Jones, founder of Enterprise Nation, there have been record-breaking spikes in start-up rates in the UK over the last few years, she said, '2012 was when the UK first hit half a million start-ups in the space of 12 months' and in 2016 '600,000 people started a limited company.'[3] These are big numbers. I give talks and workshops and get chatting to people and I'm inspired by those launching their own side-projects. I remember one workshop I did in 2016 which had such a huge variety of people in attendance, from an 87-year-old woman wanting to launch a website to sell her popular knitted items, to a 12-year-old girl who wanted to teach violin lessons over Skype to other 12-year-olds in other countries. I believe deep down we are all entrepreneurial.

We've seen the demise of the job for life and the rise in the freelance economy. The gatekeepers are gone and having so many more tools available online means we can create our own zigzag paths. We are finally asking ourselves 'Who made the rules?' when it comes to work. In the UK, we are the least productive workforce in Europe, 27 per cent less productive than our German counterparts and losing billions of pounds to productivity issues.[2] Technology has changed our lives, but it hasn't been applied to the working world as quickly as we thought it would be.

The average US office worker spends 28 per cent of the working day on emails. According to Atlassian.com (an online collaboration tool for start-ups), we spend thirty-one hours a month in unproductive meetings and 73 per cent of us do other work during those meetings.[4] According to a poll by the Chartered Management Institute covered in the *Telegraph*: 'employees are effectively cancelling out every day of their annual leave by using phones and iPads to work from home.'[5] None of this surprises me. Of course there are upsides to working in an office: face-to-face meetings, bonding with colleagues, working as a team. But I also feel that I wasted time during the day in many different ways when I worked in an office: endless cups of tea, three different radio stations on at once, 'Can I borrow you for a moment?' (when a moment turns into two hours), the aforementioned pointless meetings, unproductive delays and commutes. All these things restricted me from getting things done. We work all day in an office and then work from our phones on the commute home too, meaning our working days are longer than they should be. Studies state that our portable inbox means the working day has increased from seven and a half hours to nine and a half. So I asked myself: *What could I achieve if I designed my working days from scratch?*

I rebelled against the status quo of the traditional workplace because I felt disappointed by the inflexibility of many job roles that had no reason not to be flexible. Many companies seem so ingrained in having bums on seats and not taking into account our individual needs. Fast-forward to now: I have *many* different jobs. I am afraid I am unable to tell you what I do very easily. For a while, I felt like this was a negative thing – a lifestyle wrapped in stigma. A slashie (someone with multiple slashes in their job title) who couldn't commit to one thing. I would get tongue-tied whenever telling anyone what I did for a living. After years of mumbling instead of proudly proclaiming, I realised I wanted to write about it and like most things that you *think* are your biggest flaws, they turn out to be your biggest sell. Once I embraced this way of working and gave it a name (the Multi-Hyphen Method, of course) my life changed, as did the quality of my health and relationships, my bank balance and my idea of personal success. The Multi-Hyphen

Method has allowed me to have it all in a way I never thought possible. Sure, there are sacrifices and there are important and complex questions to be asked about the future of work (see Chapter 8), but I wanted to share my lessons and thoughts with you in this book. I wanted to write about how our home lives and work lives are merging now and how we can make that happen successfully and not burn out. Maybe you are feeling like you want a change, maybe you are braving the flexible-working question, maybe you have a side-hustle in you, maybe the job that once made you happy seems to irk you for some unexplained reason. Whatever your situation, I believe we are all multi-hyphenates deep down, we just need to be given the tools to make it physically work. We need a movement to join.

Perhaps your immediate thought is, *Ugh, having multiple strands to my career sounds like* more *work.* But this book is not about having a to-do list as long as your arm and leg, it is about allowing technology to help us do less. Tech isn't going away and we are still learning every day (which is a big theme of this method). Three decades ago, no one owned a computer in their home, now, according to research by Cisco, in 2008 there were already more 'things' connected to the Internet than people. By 2020, the amount of Internet-connected things will reach fifty billion. And there's no sign of slowing down. Certain digital skills have the ability to lessen the workload and allow us to explore other skills that interest us. Having a side-hustle is becoming a national pastime.

What if I told you that by adding many different hyphens to my career I actually work way, way fewer hours than my old nine-to-five job? Or that having multiple income streams can be a legitimate replacement for one sturdy salary? This book aims to break down the many stigmas of the modern-day work-place and explain why the hangovers of the past are ruining our chances to be fulfilled at work, keeping us feeling trapped and stopping us from embracing our many sides. This book is about how *everyone* can have an entrepreneurial mindset now and has the right to investigate it. Everyone. All we need is some tangible starting points to get our ideas off the ground and we can create new jobs, not just for ourselves but for others. It's time to break off the shackles of the traditional restrictive workplace. Who made the rules that we had to live our lives so stringently and so straight? It's a new era, a new landscape and time for new ways of working.

We also need to tackle the confidence crisis that comes with feeling like we are out there on our own battling through this era of change and forging new paths. The Internet has allowed us to hold down a job, work flexibly, create a new side-job and have a hobby if we want to, and with minimum travel require-ments. But how do we make this a bigger conversation? Why are we still scared to ask for flexibility at work and why is it still judged so harshly by many? After all, allowing ourselves to have multiple strands to our personality and careers allows us to mentally displace the weight and stresses of life on to differ-ent things instead. It's good for us. More on that later.

Recently I've found myself having long conversations with part-time cab drivers who are in the middle of launching apps, others are training to be pilots or writing books. I've met incredibly successful doctors, one who was training to be a videographer so he can be part-filmmaker when up in the mountains saving lives, another who was doing surgery one day and blogging about food the next. This isn't about being forced into gigging by companies that don't care about us and won't invest in us, this is about choosing to have multiple sides to your work that you create and getting yourself into a place where you can take full advantage of all the opportunities that come with our new in-demand culture and economy. This is about having side-projects that can be just for you. This is about empowering yourself at a time when we are becoming more and more fragile and disposable in the traditional work-place. It's about opening up these conversations and trying to make modern life work for us instead of driving us to the edge.

While being a multi-hyphenate is definitely not suited to just one generation, I couldn't help but be self-aware or at least self-analytical about where my point of view comes from as I wrote this book. I wonder if being a millennial, fighting against the label of the 'snowflake generation' and graduating during the recession of 2009 when job discovery and security was scary have become the driving force behind my work ethic. I felt like I needed a hustle on the side to make myself stand out because of the economic fear in the air and how competitive it was to secure a job. Because of serious topics like student debts and a housing crisis that affects an entire generation, I didn't think of my career in a linear way because I knew I wouldn't have the same trajectory as my baby-boomer parents. We are going to be working for a very long time and the jobs that we do will continue to change and be continuously invented.

I also knew deep in my bones that technology was evolving at such a pace that humans weren't quite keeping up with it (or knowing yet the full capacity of what we could do with it). It felt like we were sort of running alongside it. I knew work and the workplace was going to look crazily different because of the rate of technology expanding and evolving in a lifetime and that I needed to invest in myself. If nothing was secure then the only thing I could do was self-teach and invest in my own side skills. We should be taught the skills that will allow us to look at a landscape and see how it will change and grow and predict our own moves. We should be looking less inwardly when searching for a job or a career plan and instead look outward at our environment and our role within it. We should be less hung up on job titles and hierarchy and focus instead on what we can do and how much value it brings. A lot of things that used to be within a worker's control, such as steadily climbing up each rung of a career ladder, don't look the same any more, so we can't control our next five years as much as we used to be able to. We should encourage ourselves not to be thinking of our careers in a linear way. We should be praised for using 'Why?' or 'What if?' more often, instead of scorned.

Look, this idea of having multiple strands to your career isn't new. The portfolio career started to gain popularity in the 1980s and then Charles Handy popularised the idea in his book *The Empty Raincoat* (1994). But it needs drastically updating and mainstreaming. The term 'portfolio career' needs a modern twist that focuses more on tech, design and the Internet, not just having a string of random jobs loosely held together. There wasn't a book for me when I started out, a book that combined growing a portfolio with enhancing your digital skills to carve out your own success and create a lifestyle that suits you.

We all have different names for it: interdisciplinary working, slashie career, my friend Freddie calls it multi-streaming – having multiple income streams, pulling all the joint-roles together like a puppeteer. Crucially it's about making sure you do not become extinct in a workplace that is changing at lightning speed. It is diversifying yourself so that you are in the best possible position to have a long and fruitful career in a time where so much is out of our control.

I'm excited by all of this. I believe we're in a time in workplace history where our identities are made up of so many things. The phone in our bag has allowed us to daydream more than ever and connect with others effortlessly. We see everyone else's pixelated magical life and business ideas and think to ourselves: *Could I do that?* On the Internet, we are constantly reminded of our own potential and while it can be quite frightening (and sometimes overwhelming), it's also enlightening. The reason you get that fear-of-missing-out feeling when someone else starts their own business or project is because the playing field has been levelled by the Internet and you know that you could do it too. We are just as capable as Joe Bloggs. We all have similar entry points now and the opportunity to spread our message. But talk of a digital strategy is missing, in a world that is becoming more competitive and noisy by the day. We need more conversations about resources and practical starting points. Not even that long ago, you would have to walk into an IRL bank and pitch your idea and ask for a loan. We don't need that kind of permission or investment upfront any more. We can experiment, take risks, try something for almost nothing and the world will not crumble if it doesn't work because we can try these things alongside our jobs. But the point remains that we are all free to have a go.

The Multi-Hyphen Method at its heart is about being happier in walking our own paths. We've been told by society over and over again that it's totally normal to dislike our jobs. YouGov reported in 2015 that 37 per cent of British workers think their jobs are meaningless. The *Evening Standard* says 80 per cent of Londoners hate their jobs[6] and Bloomberg recently revealed that once you are over thirty-five you're more likely to hate your job.[7] I met someone at a party recently and told them I was writing this book, their response was, 'But you're *meant* to hate your job. It's a *job.*' I get it, no job is perfect all the time, but having multiple strings to your bow allows your life to be less weighted on one thing. Dispersing yourself and straddling multiple interests will make you better at each one because you are constantly improving and being challenged in multiple ways. You feel less trapped. You get to leapfrog over old barriers. It means you are giving yourself a break by embracing different parts of your life – personality and career.

I wanted to write a book that proves that anyone can bring in extra money or create personal value via online means and how this can empower us. We just need to be given the tools to know where to start. We assume that if we are in a vibrant city we are getting the most opportunities – and that is true of networking events – but you don't have to be a city-dwelling millennial to be an early adopter of new technology. For example, Laura Mudie started Rosa & Bo (a colourful range of nursery products) in Southend-on-Sea on the side of her day job as a midwife and Julie Deane and her mother Freda started the Cambridge Satchel Company at their kitchen table. You can create something interesting and engaging online no matter where you reside. This is its power. This is your potential for more freedom.

The Multi-Hyphen Method will offer you a different approach to your work life. It's the career guide I wish I'd had.

This book is about making yourself *more* employable in an ever-changing and unpredictable world. It's about unpicking the stories we tell ourselves about who we are and our relationship with work. It's about overcoming any fears about it being dog eat dog online and offline. It's about playing to your strengths and defining your own success. It is going to bust the myths that there is only room for one job in our lives. It's about creating career longevity in a world and workplace that still has many hangovers from the past. It is about creating *more* stability for ourselves, not less, so that you are employable not just over the next few years, but the next few decades of unpredictability. It's about using one of the greatest gifts we've been given – the Internet – and working towards a flexible future.

CHAPTER 1

Dictionary Definition of Success vs [Insert Your Own]

SUCCESS

səkˈsɛs/

noun

1. the accomplishment of an aim or purpose
    - the attainment of fame, wealth, or social status
    - a person or thing that achieves desired aims or attains
      fame, wealth, etc.[1]

In the dictionary, under the broad definition of success, which is to 'accomplish an aim or purpose' (makes sense, sure), there is also the more sinister definition that creeps into our culture: *'a person or thing that achieves desired aims or attains fame, wealth, etc.'*. It's the definition of success that we are fed in the media, on billboards, on TV and in advertising, constantly. The Internet memes and TV adverts that still perpetuate the idea that we will be happier if we have more money, more things, more recognition or more social-media followers. We will be a better version of ourselves if we get a bit famous! Or if we have loads of money, things, grand fireplaces, expensive rugs, gold and jewels! I, like many people I'm sure, fell into this trap at some point, thinking that all my problems would be fixed if I became 'successful' in this way. This definition still lingers. Recognition and validation feel good. Initially.

But it's time to create a definition for ourselves. There are so many different ways to live your life, run your business and earn your money. I am a multi-hyphenate, meaning that on paper I might not look as successful as someone sat at a shiny desk in a tall, expensive building with a marble lobby. But having a multi-hyphenate career innately means you are forced to create your own definition of success and you can't directly compare yourself to others. It's about carving your own path and staying in that lane. Your career mixture will look entirely different to someone else's, even if you have similar jobs. It's your bespoke package.

There are lots of things that are so ingrained in what we *think* success is that I have to force myself to inspect it and question it instead of just going along with it. *Is that* my *definition of success?* I ask myself. What do I actually want to do with my life? I can feel successful in the most mundane of moments, where I've made it through the day, not had any significant dramas and then had a cup of tea on the sofa. I can also feel successful when I've been paid handsomely for my work. There are many different definitions of success that can apply to each of my individual career strands. It's up to us to start figuring it out, instead of chasing after the glamourised messages we absorb through media, be it social or traditional.

It's totally fine to have different definitions of success to your family, friends, peers or strangers on the Internet. For example, I was recently pitched a guest for my podcast show – these sorts of pitches appear most days in my inbox. I love hearing from and getting the chance to meet and interview new people who I might never have come across before. One pitch recently had me scratching my head though, the email read:

Dear Emma,

I have a suggestion for your podcast. We think you should interview X, an incredibly successful businessman, who made so much money he retired at 26. Would you like to hear how he did it?

This jarred with me and I couldn't work out why at first. Was this *the* definition of success? Working and then retiring early? The thing is, it wasn't my definition. We are bought and sold success stories on a daily basis. We're constantly told that we should be successful and *young*. But no one is young forever. Success has no chance of surviving through your life if being young in your career is fetishised. Did I want to add to the gloss and romanticisation of this idea of success? I am far more interested in discussing longevity – a life full of twists and turns and ups and downs and career changes. Balance. Fulfilment. Staying active, enjoying life. Working a healthy amount. And yes, of course retiring (I hope) at some point! A corporate job and early retirement wasn't *my* definition (though still a valid one), so I realised it was also up to me to push back on a few definitions of success and hold them to account before I followed along. Each to our own. I knew I wanted to design a lifestyle that worked for me and not necessarily climb the traditional ladder striving for promotion after promotion and feeling deflated at the end. I wanted to make sure I was having fun and fulfilling myself as I grew along the way. I wanted to enjoy my work, the challenges, the reinventions, the evolution and the dance of a career and a life lived my way.

In her book *Lean In* Sheryl Sandberg dismisses the career ladder and instead calls it the career 'jungle gym'.[2] Essentially, it's all about monkey-barring your way to your new role. And as Kara Melchers, managing editor of BITE (a marketing trends agency) said: 'Our destination is not always reached by a ladder. In my head it's more like a climbing frame, one with tunnels and slides and ropes; as long as you're enjoying the journey, you're going in the right direction.'[3]

Switching things up and trying new things is becoming less of a stigma, thankfully. I remember a boss at my old workplace telling me to stick each job out for two years otherwise you look unreliable to recruiters. Now, I don't think that's true. And even if you want to stay within a company, there are so many positives to side-stepping within the building. The study posted on LinkedIn by Guy Berger called 'How to Become an Executive' analysed all the different ways people reached the top of their careers and achieved success in those roles. LinkedIn scanned data from 459,000 of their global members who worked at big consulting companies over a twenty-year period and were in senior positions. The study results showed that those who worked across multiple departments at a particular job had a surprising win over other colleagues who stayed in just one role or department. It showed that being adaptable, taking on different roles and adding new strings to your bow became a huge advantage in the workplace.

It's important that we embrace this zigzag route and not see it as 'less than' in comparison to the traditional career ladder.

Adam Smiley Poswolsky, author of *The Quarter-Life Breakthrough: Invent Your Own Path, Find Meaningful Work, And Build A Life That Matters* said (to *Glamour* magazine):

> Changes in technology mean that people can't count on a position, or even a company, being around forever. Think of your career as a pond of lily pads spread out in all directions. This doesn't mean you should quit your job every six months for another lily pad, but it does mean that, to remain competitive, you have to become good at one thing, and then another thing, and figure out where those two skills intersect to add more value to your company.[4]

I never did understand why 'jack of all trades' was always meant as some sort of insult, because it's becoming more and more apparent that a diverse CV is more powerful as you grow and thrive in your career. You can be an expert in multiple things.

The Rise of Online 'Success Porn'

If you've ever read a motivational quote that feels disingenuous or seen a picture of an office space with a marble desk and velvet chaise longue posted on Instagram, they can be labelled under 'motivational porn' or 'success porn'. It's the way people try and get your attention by pornifying the idea of success, hyping you up, making you want more, but with no real satisfaction at the end. There are over ten thousand uses of the hashtag #deskporn on Instagram and it appears to be on the rise. One of my most disliked #workporn memes is the one that says 'I'd rather hustle 24/7 than slave nine-to-five '. It's shared on Pinterest *a lot*. The idea of hustling 24/7 is a really dangerous mentality to share, as working non-stop is not conducive to our happiness. We shouldn't be dividing our options into two extremes (i.e. nine-to-five = set hours vs self-employment = working round the clock). There is a middle ground between working nine-to-five and working 24/7. You *can* work towards creating your own ratio.

If success porn in the fifties was a corner office and in the nineties it was Steve Jobs quotes, then in 2018 it is the Mac-owning Instagrammable #GirlBoss running her empire from a beach in Bali. Although technology has allowed us to carve a new path for ourselves in the shape of a new side-hustle, we are bombarded with other people's 'successes' daily: someone else's successful kids, a successful moving-house date, a successful job promotion, a successful relationship, a success-ful shopping trip. We are inundated with other people's lives. Or at least a very small part of people's public lives. Even though the Internet is responsible for a positive upheaval of our working lives, it is also the breeding ground for making us feel like everyone else is more successful than us. It takes a nanosecond to go from being okay with your life to spiralling downward into total compare and despair mode.

We can now access a new online world of endless pixelated lives and examples of success and make life choices based on what we see and think we want. We are influenced by so many more things now. Tech has gone from being something we choose to use, to something we cannot escape. There are now so many platforms for people to showcase their success (albeit the highlight reel) and there are more tools to be successful on. The things we see and scroll through can change our minds and disrupt our true callings. To paint a picture of how quickly things have moved, in 2006 these things didn't exist:

* iPhone (and apps!)
* 4G
* Android
* WhatsApp
* Netflix
* Bitcoin
* Instagram
* Uber
* Snapchat
* Spotify
* Kickstarter

The list goes on. We are inundated with information. Slowing down and sitting back isn't just important for our mental and physical health, it also allows us to see the wood for the trees. Are you really chasing your own 'success', or someone else's? There's never been a better time than now to recalibrate our own definitions of success.

Work is Personal and Emotional

Work is an emotional subject for so many reasons. It can affect our mood, our perception of self-worth and in some cases, our health. Not everyone loves their job. In fact, if you do, you are the exception. According to Monster, 76 per cent of workers get Sunday-night blues stressing out about the following day.[5] You're thought to be very lucky if you enjoy your job but often the reality of finding yourself in a job you love is a result of many sacrifices along the way, one of which being an incredibly low starting wage and working for free or 'exposure' in order to beat an overwhelming amount of competition from all corners. In order to 'do what you love' it is thought that you have to cut back on the comfortable job security, go without stability and take a lot of risks. I was talking with friends of mine recently about just how controversial it can be at times to be the person who is happy at work. It can make things awkward in a friendship if you clearly love your job and your friends hate theirs. You may have uncomfortable conversations with friends who don't have the career they desire but they might not want to take the leap or to earn less during a transition period either.

When I set out in the working world I was slightly jealous of friends who were lawyers or recruiters who enjoyed big salaries, luxurious holidays and fancy restaurants right at the very beginning of their careers, whereas I was on £11k a year trying to break into an industry I was passionate about but was known to pay pretty badly. But I soon learned it really is a waste of time comparing yourself to others when the decisions you made from the start were different.

It's easy to feel hard done by. Privileged connections and nepotism can be hard to stomach when you are first starting out. It's a really tricky, sticky subject and it affects us all. Which is why it's more important than ever to have an understanding of the future of technology and the future of work, so that obstacles can be examined more closely and we can overcome them no matter our background or starting point. The old-fashioned CV, for example, used to be a way to manually filter who was and wasn't the right fit based on background information. Now, the work can speak for itself and instead of a CV, your side-hustle, project or your website appearing on a certain Google search result could win you the job. According to a new CareerBuilder survey, 70 per cent of employers use social media to snoop on potential candidates before hiring them. It's even got a name – social recruiting – and three in ten employers have someone solely dedicated to scrolling through the online profiles of prospective employees to find new, exciting hires based on the work published online.

Educating ourselves, empowering ourselves with tech and learning how to be more visible online can lift up voices that used to not be listened to at all. We can all be more visible now. The resurgence of podcasts, for example, has meant a new voice or an idea can reach thousands if not millions of listeners, without needing to go through the gatekeepers of radio stations. It's pretty great to have direct access to an audience.

SOME WAYS IN WHICH THE INTERNET HAS LEVELLED THE PLAYING FIELD

- We get to choose how many hours we put into a side hobby, as we all have access to the tools to build the starting points of a business.
- Anyone can build up an audience and communicate with them, rivalling traditional media outlets.
- Flexible new start-ups can enable new parents to start their own business from home.

- Up-to-date tech and tools, on the whole, are accessible in most homes.
- In a time of change, companies and clients are willing to take risks on new, upcoming talent.
- The growth of self-published audio. For example, 4.7 million adults in the UK have listened to any type of podcast.[6]

Being a Multi-Hyphenate is About Building *Your* Own Definition of Success

'What I know now that I didn't know at 21 is that life is a series of dreams realised. There is no destination, but there will be breakthrough after breakthrough along the way. Our greatest obligation is to keep reaching, to continue growing, to push beyond what seems possible, to live outside the boxes created for us.' – Elaine Welteroth, former editor of *Teen Vogue*[7]

So we know that the research tells us we are unhappy in our working lives. Further research done by the London School of Business and Finance (LSBF) shows us that we're not taking this lightly. The study found that 2.8 million people quit their jobs monthly. According to HRReview.co.uk it costs a load of money to replace members of staff who leave suddenly and train up someone new – £30,614 per employee to be exact. By having more flexibility, more joyful moments at work and realising that we can sometimes like our string of jobs we could save this wastage of money and have more opportunities for growth, personally and professionally.

A multi-hyphenate career means drawing on the things you find interesting and/or are good at and creating your own career puzzle. It's like going into a career Build-a-Bear Workshop store. This takes reflection and analysis of what you enjoy, what you are good at, what you can build on, what you can enhance online and ultimately what you can sell. The reason the multi-hyphenate lifestyle suits so many of us is because we are saying goodbye to the idea that you have to fit into one box. The Internet has allowed us to live a dual life in a way – an impressive virtual self brings more IRL opportunities along with it. It is now crucial to have an online and offline portfolio of work.

Author Neville Hobson summed it up well in this line on his website (NevilleHobson.com): 'In a job-dissolving world, self-worth replaces identity.'[8] We are losing our career identities because old status jobs are disappearing, so we have to find self-worth from other sources.

Status – and therefore 'success' – used to be all about hours spent in the office, an expensive outfit, good hair, how extroverted you were and how much money you earned. However, modern-day success is not one-size-fits-all – and it never has been. The Internet is allowing us to explore other parts of our personality and interests. Having many possessions appears to have lost its meaning a bit too – we don't have as many *things*. We curate our digital lives with things, but the idea of material possessions being the definition of success is fading, with people valuing experiences and memories (neither of which are created in meetings) over material goods. According to the research, millennials in the UK rank going travelling and having experiences as a higher financial priority over the next five years than buying a car or home, or paying off debt.

There is a tension between how the Internet can allow us to be individual, explore our passions and interests and tap into the tribes that share common interests with us while also being the largest breeding ground for buzzwords and trends, some of which can be really fickle and short-lasting. On the Internet something is immediately 'cool' and everybody jumps on board. For example, trends like clean-eating or extreme digital detoxing can take over the virtual space and can mean that we get easily confused with what it is that we actually want and what it is that actually makes us happy. We start following and aspiring to a trend that we see others socially reward and validate. Social media is jarring because of this – we aspire to lifestyles of 'successful' people but there's very little transparency around what those lifestyles demand or where they come from. We see people getting paid to travel the world, but what are the sacrifices being made? What is the day-to-day like? How was the travel funded in the first place? We don't see this sort of backstory on Instagram. We are tricked into thinking other people's successes are easy to come by and we can feel deflated instead of doing important things to further our own success. Social-media connection can be too shallow, exchanging likes and compliments when really we should be sharing more resources.

Our social and cultural idea of 'success' over the years has been: be good at something as a child, do well in your exams, go to a good university, get a stable job, get promoted, keep getting promoted, get a bit more money, get engaged, get married, have children, retire, pension, die. (Fun.)

Or as David Brent (Ricky Gervais's character in *The Office*) says: 'You grow up, you work half a century, you get a golden handshake, you rest a couple of years, then you're dead.'

We are all fed an idea of what our lives will be when we grow up. Most of us are told at school to achieve and be ambitious, whether that's at home or in the workplace. In recent decades, women have been told to 'Have it all'. It's dangerous for success to be directly correlated to ambition. I have friends who admit (whispering like they are telling a dirty secret) that they have realised they just aren't that ambitious in the traditional sense when it comes to work. It shouldn't be seen as a bad thing to not be ambitious. I look at their lives, albeit different to mine (with babies, gardens, more free time) and I think to myself how much they have nailed their own version of success. They are incredibly successful.

It's great that women are now seen as capable human beings in the workplace (wow thanks!) but it's worth remembering that being able to have the *same* opportunity is not the same as wanting the same thing. But as women in the UK are still paid 22.6 per cent less per hour than men it's hard for money not to be wrapped up in our measure of success and to push for more. We don't want fulfilment and feeling purposeful at work – which are emotional traits normally pinned on women – to end up as being excuses for paying women less. I wouldn't want anyone to pay me less just because they are assuming that I'm feeling really fulfilled by the opportunity. It is assumed that women are more likely to be happy doing caring jobs over men, but we want and deserve straight-up cash too. According to OECD.org, around the globe women spend two to ten times more time on unpaid care work than men. Some women don't want to be ambitious, just as some men don't. We all want different things and that's okay. But we shouldn't be stereotyped into certain roles or have any decisions made based on gender. Success is personal.

Inward vs Outward Success

In many ways we as a society are incredibly lucky. If we were working in the nineteenth century, we would be shackled to a machine and our work (and the hours) would depend on our gender and background. We are able to forge new paths for ourselves and technology and the Internet can help us jump through hoops, meaning our work is less labour-intensive.

The traditional office space is a hangover from the Industrial Revolution too, when people had to be together for daylight hours to talk to their colleagues and use machinery that wasn't portable. Even the apparently modern open-plan office isn't that modern. According to The Debrief, the open-plan office is thought to have originated in Germany in the 1950s

from the idea of Bürolandschaft (office landscape). It was based on the work of the brutalist architect Frank Lloyd Wright. It was adopted by businesses all over the world, and is now generally accepted as a utopian dream for businesses and their workers. However, after half a century of open plan living, people are starting to question whether it really is the best way to work.[9]

The open-plan office gives the illusion of flexibility (with hot-desking seen as a perk) but it is not modern in terms of the technology we now have to hand in other areas of our lives. It's still a place that practises looking busy over constantly being busy. Face-to-face is still very important for relationship-building, but we are still physically shackled way more than we need to be. We don't all find the same spaces productive but this is hardly ever taken into account. In one survey, 58 per cent of high-performance employees said they need more quiet work spaces.[10] Another survey, conducted by Canada Life Group Insurance, found that people who work in open-plan offices took over 70 per cent more sick days than those who worked at home.[11]

While doing some research, I found a *Huffington Post* article which stated that it was still possible that we could actually be fired for coming in an hour late to work. Seems a bit harsh, no? Obviously you must tell your colleagues if you're running late, but this seemed a good example of this rigid bums-on-seats mentality that is killing our energy, happiness and lifestyles. In this article, it gives a case study of Michelle Edwards, who says 'she called in one hour late to work, telling her boss she needed to care for her mother, recovering from surgery. But the boss' response was that she was already fired for "no call, no show," according to the lawsuit Edwards filed against her employer, Advanced Temporaries Inc.'[12] With all these flexibility tools at our fingertips, why would being a bit late still be treated as such an awful workplace crime in a traditional office set-up when we can do a lot of desk work from anywhere? When we can easily make up hours outside of the office from any location? Of course there is a distinction to be made between being late for no reason and not being granted a flexible start time.

But it seems on the whole we aren't using our time as wisely as we could be because many old rules are getting in the way and they are not really benefiting work productivity.

Another hangover from the past is workplace martyrdom. A workplace martyr is someone who is sat at their desk at 10 p.m. not doing much, maybe watching a YouTube video, but wanting to complain about how late it is and how busy they are and how long their to-do list is. It used to be really impressive to be stuck in the office until 11 p.m. (I was definitely that person!) This is also referred to as presenteeism, the definiton being 'the practice of being present at one's place of work for more hours than is required'. My opinion of what constitutes a successful working day has swung totally the other way, it is now getting good work done in the *least* amount of time.

It's interesting to look at the workplace martyr in different situations and different cultures. For example, in Japan, according to the labour ministry, few workers come even close to taking their full quota of holiday.[13] In South Korea it's encouraged to go for drinks and dinner with colleagues at least two nights a week. On average, due to this social requirement, South Koreans consume fourteen shots of hard liquor a week as part of workplace culture.[14] In the Netherlands it is frowned upon if you work late. There, friends don't think, *Wow, you work really hard, you have an amazing high-powered job.* They think, *What are you doing wrong?* Or, *You must not be very good at your job if you need to stay later.* In the UK a lot of us are workaholics by nature and think that staying late can earn us brownie points from the boss. According to research by Fellowes, in the UK over half of employees go into work when sick, which is presenteeism at its worst. It's even more extreme in the US. According to a U.S. Travel Association survey, 41 per cent of Americans don't take their paid time off, which is pretty alarming. It's interesting that each culture can have its own version of what success is, which the culture and society follow sometimes without realising. These are still things that exist in our journey in wanting to become 'successful' in the eyes of our colleagues and acquaintances around us. The rise of individualism is not met without criticism but the rise in individualistic tendencies (not just in the West but globally according to studies) at least might mean that employees are more likely to start looking inward and realise a sense of personal worth over outward perceptions.

These rigid definitions of success are way past their sell-by date. There is an alternative definition of success which I am presenting in this book and that is living a balanced, enriched life by having multiple careers or interests. The Internet has created many different access points for us too. There's no right way to navigate towards your dream situation. We don't need to conform to old versions of success however entrenched in our culture they might seem. We don't have to have one job for life. We don't have to choose one impressive career path and stick to it. We can have any ratio or career mix. We can have multiple job streams, we can have side-hustles, we can have many different definitions of who we are and how we want to live. We can step off the collective hamster wheel. It's okay if we can't sum up what we do easily, it's okay if we don't wow anyone at a dinner party with our job title, it's okay if what we do doesn't fit into the traditional version of success. If we build a lifestyle that works for *us*.

What Success *Used* to Mean to Me

When I look back to what success meant to me as a young child, it was never about grades or marks or stars. I think I was just lazy and was totally happy doing the bare minimum to scrape by. I almost thrived on the art of doing just enough. I never cared about being one of those academic overachievers or praise from teachers. I hardly ever got any gold stars, certificates or trophies for being number one but on the upside, it also meant there was no anxiety or pressure to maintain any sort of special title. There is a pressure once you are successful to then *maintain* that success. It is one loose theory as to why so many famous young actors go off the rails, they are celebrated incessantly for their big successes and then a dry career spell can send them into a downward spiral because they feel they have lost something. In my childhood eyes, it definitely made more sense to be mediocre at something and then you don't get people's expectations set too high. If you did, you were sure to disappoint someone later down the line. Turned out that not being competitive is an easy way to get by and reduce anxiety. I actively avoided most classroom competition and instead chose to remain averagely happy and perform well socially. I was the same with board games. I would see someone getting dramatically competitive and richer than me over a game of Monopoly and just count my $1 notes. I just didn't care.

As I got older and into my teens, I started to develop a different definition of success, which for me was based on popularity. It wasn't about being clever, but having the most social attention. I would feel on a high and skip home if someone popular allowed me to sit next to them or gave me their last

Rolo or picked me to be in their sports team. Social situations were always what made me feel successful. If I was invited to the cool party, I felt puffed up, if I was offered a cigarette by the older, cool kids, I felt a million dollars. In some ways, this is still my definition. I never feel more successful than when I'm surrounded by good, interesting people at work or friends I've kept close to me for decades.

When I moved to London aged twenty-one, I expected to plod along. I was just happy that I was in London and managing to survive and stay alive in one of the world's most expensive cities. I wanted to be a writer but that could wait. I just wanted to get any job, be okay at it and go home on time. That was enough. But then that started to change.

Via my side-hustles and my blog taking off, I started to get invited to the 'in' parties and people began to tell me I was successful. The thing is, being seen as successful through other people's eyes (and not necessarily your own) can be addictive. You are rewarded if you become successful by society's (often shallow) standards and through online means. We become validated by likes and comments. We know that getting online attention can be as addictive as dopamine. Likes and comments feel just as good as sex, drugs and a really good hug. I became obsessed with getting more and more positive feedback on my apparent and visual success. It started to empower me, control me and sort of take over. I wasn't in competition with others, I was in competition with myself. I was in competition with the last successful thing I'd done. You start to chase your own tail and keeping up with your unrealistic goals you start setting for yourself can be exhausting.

Fast-forward to now. What does success mean to me?

Someone said that success to them was having enough flexibility that you can take yourself to a midweek matinee performance at the theatre. Freedom is important to me. People want to feel free, even if it's as simple as being left to do menial tasks your way. When FlexJobs surveyed 2,600 office employees in August 2015, the majority said they actually prefer doing their most important tasks outside of the office.[15]

When I look back through my experiences I genuinely feel successful when I think of the network of people I have around me. I have friendships that have lasted decades. I feel successful in that I have time, time to work on my relationships like any other project, time to reflect, time to travel, time to take an afternoon off. And I have enough money to live.

The ability to have more flexible working, to work on my own side-projects, add different themes and strands to my work and personal identity and use those playful skills that were lost once I became an adult have all added to my personal definition of success. Outwardly, success can look quite small, but the personal inward feeling can be ginormous. The Multi-Hyphen Method is a new way of expanding our horizons, not feeling trapped and realising that each of us has multiple roles to play in the world.

What Does Success Mean to You?

Success. A word wrapped up with so many different connotations, ideas, subconscious preconceptions. Does success *actually* still mean what we've been told it must mean? How do we take back control and pinpoint our own definition to keep for ourselves?

Before writing down your own definition, sometimes reading other people's thoughts can inspire you. **Success to me is . . .**

LOTTIE, *PR manager* (Millennial)

'Being trusted, respected and having my work recognised. Being able to be authentic (working with people and projects I genuinely think are exciting or credible). Making things happen that I would genuinely enjoy regardless of work makes me really happy. Nothing demotivates me like working on something that I either don't think is credible or I don't feel a connection to.'

ANA, *magazine editor* (Gen X)

'The meaning has really changed over the years. I don't know if it's a combination of getting older (and, hopefully, wiser . . .) and having a daughter, but the image I had of myself of flying between cities, owning a couple of apartments around the world and living the glamorous, dreamed-up life of an international journalist is no longer my definition of success. It was a life focused around work, where success was measured by how much time you spent working and how much money you made – and it was all centred on you, you, you. Now, my values have changed. Success is partly linked to work, but it goes beyond the superficial. At work, I care about nurturing my team. I care about the actual work I'm doing. Am I making a difference? Sometimes, and when I do, however small that difference might be, for me, success is being true to my values – and having the courage to live by them.'

SARA, *hospice counsellor – supervisor-baker* (Baby boomer)

'Success to me is about doing paid work that has meaning and allows me autonomy to decide how I work. There's an element of public recognition and knowing I am respected especially by my professional peers. I want to be paid enough so that I'm not constantly worrying about money and there's enough for a few treats. I always want another level to achieve and more things to learn. Success for me is not a destination but a state of being that requires maintenance.'

NATALIA, *visual artist* (Millennial)

'It took me a long time to define this for myself (and I still struggle a bit), but I definitely feel most "successful" when I make a decision confidently and without any of the noise in life distracting me, and execute said decision; be it a work-based decision or a life one. It's about all my feelings coming from deep within, not bounced off someone else. So as long as I feel happy with a choice I have made and something I have done, I think it's a success.'

SOPHIE, *content manager* (Millennial)

'This is something I've thought about a lot having had four careers already (journalism, clinical psychology, charity/digital stuff, podcasting!). When I was younger I think success related to recognition (i.e. people seeing your name in print). As I've got older I've understood it's much more to do with being happy and enjoying what you do, whatever that is.'

ALEX, *catering – company founder* (Gen X)

'At the moment success means getting the right work-life balance which enables me to manage my business with the energy and passion required. I also feel that success can be as simple as still being in business! Catering can be a tough old game and as long as I am in business and managing to make some money I suppose I am successful! (Blush!)'

GEORGIE, *property manager* (Millennial)

'Oooh that's tough to pinpoint. Success is pushing above and beyond the boundaries, not only personally but also what society considers to be a certain level of success for people my age/for women(!). Being promoted to a senior level in a quicker time frame than others, being younger than other managers/ directors, being continually promoted within a fairly heavy male industry, financial security, personal happiness, pride in what you do and respect from those around you.'

LIZZIE, *founder of agency The Hoxby Collective* (Gen X)

'Loving what I do, and being true to my work style – whatever it may be at that particular time. I'm a big believer that everyone should be deeply passionate about what they do and fulfilled in their lives, be that their work, families or hobbies. I think people being fulfilled in their work specifically will make for a happier (and also more productive) society as a whole and that people should keep reflecting and questioning what they do and how they work until they truly feel happy with it – it's never too late for a change. Everyone should also be able to fit their work around their lives rather than the other way round.'

RACHEL, *founder of headhunting agency Talent Atelier* (Gen X)

'Having the time to actually reflect on what I've achieved – if I was just constantly working and never talking a step back then I don't think success would ever be attainable. It can come in so many forms, but often I don't realise what I've achieved unless someone reminds me, which is totally daft. They're like, "Hey, you've got your own business with employees and it's super cool" and I'm sitting there like, "Oh yeah!" Success can be a total pain in the arse though as the likelihood is that if you're an entrepreneur you suffer from impostor syndrome and probably won't be able to take in what you've done. It might be a couple of seconds where you're happy but then you are on to the next thing . . .'

KATE, WRITER – *author of The Friendship Cure* (Millennial)

'I've been thinking about this a lot lately – and finding myself caring significantly less about my definition of success from, say, a decade ago. I seem to have recalibrated my ambition and where it used to be about the big, classic signs of success like a very obvious career on TV/radio, it's more personal now, like doing cool stuff that makes me feel inspired. It feels like a more sensible, less frenzied form of success that I'm after now – more closely aligned to happiness and creativity than the appearances of great things. So success to me now is being engaged with awesome people I respect, getting to do work I care about and looking forward to a long, interesting career (rather than getting somewhere big fast fast fast). I'm actually starting to grasp that I will be working for decades to come so success needn't come in a hurry – it's more to do with having great things to do for a long time.'

GRACE, *documentary maker – campaigner* (Gen Z)

'It really depends on the mood I'm in, and how secure I'm feeling in myself. Sometimes, when I'm feeling comfortable in my body, and in life, I judge success on how happy I am while I'm working with people I get on well with, which is most of the time. But then on other days, when I'm mentally low, fearing death, and comparing myself to other people around me, I feel like I need to get nominated for an Oscar and a BAFTA all at once to prove to myself that I'm talented.'

LIV, *writer – blogger* (Gen Z)

'Ultimately being happy and the feeling of contentment. Not feeling stressed by my career and being able to put food on the table without a burgeoning pressure. It's also meant to be able to create my own career and support myself in a creative industry. Once it was all about numbers and keeping up with the Joneses, but I think as I get older it's been easier to appreciate what actually makes me feel successful, content and fulfilled.'

Practical Exercises

What are your definitions of success? Write down how your definition of success has changed from being a child, to a teen, to an adult. What needs to change or be tweaked? What has more or less weight now on your overall happiness and satisfaction? What definitions have you got rid of? Which parts of your life make you feel like you're the most fulfilled? What part of your life makes you feel the most successful and why?

Another good exercise is to write down a list of things that maybe look good on paper, but don't matter so much *to you* personally. Write the list and then physically draw a line through each one.

The benefits of figuring out your definition of success and writing them down enables you to feel secure in your own personal definition that won't match anyone else's like for like. It means you have a version to keep to yourself, which you don't ever need to share if you don't want to. It means you are less likely to compare yourself to others, because they might be on track to meet their version, but your actions may look entirely different to meet your own specific requirements for *your* success.

How to make your own pie chart: The idea is to keep a list over a few weeks, or months, of all the things that make you feel balanced. On days where you go to bed thinking 'that was a good day', write down the things you did. It might surprise you how small the action or output might be. Like cooking a good meal, hitting a deadline, buying a good birthday present for someone, spending time on your hobby or getting a pay rise. Whatever it is, write it down. The key is to write down the things that genuinely make you feel good, *not just* what you think will look good on paper. Then, take all these, group them into categories (i.e. if you have lots of references to time away from your desk, perhaps this can become 'travel'), and assign them a percentage of how important they are to you.

Keep this pie chart above your desk, stuck to your laptop or in a notebook you use often so you are reminded of it. I re-evaluate mine once a year. It gives enough perspective on what you have achieved and the ways in which you might have changed.

Here's mine (which is ever-changing, and that's okay too!)

My Version of Success

A sense of creative fulfilment (20%)

Hearing positive feedback from people I admire (10%)

Being able to afford a new throw for the sofa (5%)

Being able to travel (15%)

Spending time on my own well-being (25%)

Seeing my friends and family (25%)

CHAPTER 2

Generations and Motivations

'It is one of the great ironies of life that each generation believes its experiences are unique.' – John Mauldin, financial expert and New York Times bestselling author[1]

Different generations have always felt distanced from each other. The challenge is not to stereotype. But it's hard. Immediate stereotypes spring to mind as I type this. I can't help it: younger generations appear threatening to me, older generations can seem wise but also intensely judgemental at times. But it doesn't make sense to be labelled and put into boxes simply based on the year we were born.

Those within the same generation each grow up with a slightly different set of circumstances but will always have some similarities with the people who were born in the same year or decade. After all, we are all products of our environment and the economy we grow up in.

But what are the generational differences? Here I take a look at the different motivations each generation has and how the years in which they were born could inform some of their work ethic and careers and also how they define success.

Generational Overview[2]

• THE SILENT GENERATION (1925–45)

The Silent Generation's work ethic is extremely strong and obedient. According to TheBalance.com it's because this generation were supposed to be 'seen and not heard'.[3]

'They are highly dedicated and the most risk averse. Their values were shaped by the Great Depression, World War II, and the postwar boom years. Silents possess a 'strong commitment to teamwork and collaboration and have high regard for developing interpersonal communications skills', according to training company Amanet.

• BABY BOOMERS (1943–64)

Baby Boomers are called this because they are the result of the 'boom' of new babies post World War II. They are the first generation to on the whole do better financially than their parents. According to TheBalance.com: 'in the early years of the boom, schools were overcrowded, colleges didn't have enough seats, and the competition for starting jobs was intense. As a result, the young Baby Boomers learned to compete for resources and success.' They are also more open to changing things up and are less rigid and obedient than their parents' generation. 'They are more optimistic and open to change than the prior generation, but they are also responsible for the "Me Generation," with its pursuit of personal gratification,' according to training company Amanet.

• GEN X (1961–80)

The label for this generation became popular alongside Douglas Copeland's book *Generation X – Tales For An Accelerated Culture*. Millennials grew up on the Internet, Generation X created it. Gen X 'naturally question authority figures and are responsible for creating the work/life balance concept. Born in a time of declining population growth, this generation of workers possesses strong technical skills and is more independent than the prior generations', according to training company Amanet.

• MILLENNIALS (1982–2004)

Millennials or Gen Y are 'the first global-centric generation, having come of age during the rapid growth of the Internet and an increase in global terrorism', according to training company Amanet. Having grown up online during their early teens they had 'significant gains in technology and an increase in educational programming during the 1990s, the Millennials are also the most educated generation of workers today.'

• GEN Z (2000–2014)[4]

Gen Z are pretty new to the workplace but have had all sorts of Internet hobbies for years as they've pretty much always been online. They will most likely go into jobs that aren't yet invented, and care about having a purpose and participating in social activism. According to entrepreneur.com 'they have also grown up in a much more accepting and respectful environment compared to those generations that came before.'

A Few Obvious Generational Differences

When I think of the divide between my parents and me, I don't feel like we live that differently on a micro level. According to reports, baby boomers are now the fastest-growing group of social-media adopters, but my job didn't exist when they had jobs, so I can't ask for granular advice because the jobs market has changed so fast and they are now retired. We differ in our relationship to university (my fees were huge, my dad went for free) and the housing markets we experienced were different too. But our gap is much narrower in some ways than my dad's and my grandad's generational divide. I can talk to my dad about most things, he is tech-savvy (and can ask Alexa to play music from his Sonos speakers), he understands the struggles of my generation when it comes to the smaller details and we have a lot of things in common. My dad's dad, however, of the Silent Generation, had no real education, left school at fourteen to work in a butcher's shop, then fought in the war and never ever had a computer or a mobile phone. There are so many things he did that I will never be able to relate to.

So you could argue that the gaps between generations are becoming smaller. Are we more bonded because of the similar tech we use? Will the first digital-native generation (aka millennials) be closer to their digital-native children? It will be the first time a 100 per cent digital native will give birth to another digital native, after all. We are moving in the same worlds, but there will still be divides because of how fast technology moves on.

Arguably, our working structures have remained pretty much the same for decades and decades, since the Silent

Generation. When you think of just how much has changed between the Silent Gen and Gen Z, it's crazy that work hasn't changed in leaps and bounds to reflect that. The nine-to-five and bums-on-seats mentality is still rewarding loyalty, which is what the Silent Gen was known for, over and above productivity. We still put face-to-face contact high on the priority list, like the Silent Generation, which is important but not as necessary as it once was when no technology existed at all. We are a million miles away from what work used to look like, so how do we change up the face of work, especially for new generations?

Why Do We Keep Pitting Generations Against Each Other?

When any system has been in place for a long time, there are hangovers (and not the alcoholic kind) that we have to deal with. The residue of any old system still lingers even if it seems like big changes have been made over time. It can be messy and uncomfortable. The millennial generation and younger don't think too positively of the old rules of the workplace, mainly because they seem outdated compared with the rapidly updating technology and tools. Millennials experimented and were early adopters of new under-the-radar tech for years before getting a job, so perhaps find it jarring when they feel they can't put their niche digital knowledge to really good use and instead have to adhere to systems, hierarchies and old structures. Millennials don't necessarily remember the good old days as they graduated around the time of the recession and so weren't yet a solid part of the working world when print magazines had a load of money to play with or when the music industry was still thriving selling hard copies or when we only shopped on the high street. Perhaps this is why they are more adaptable and are happy to get on with things in new ways or start their own ventures from scratch entirely due to the lack of nostalgia for a more traditionally stable time and with not much to lose. But it's not just millennials who want to change up the workplace or work in a multi-hyphenate way.

It's crazy to think we have five different generations at work right now, spanning from age seventeen to seventy. Of course this will mean similarities and differences in work opinion, career history and values. It's all about finding each other's strengths and not making assumptions about people based on what generation they are from and being sensitive to any workplace tensions.

Many companies I worked at were brimming with new roles in digital departments and I found myself managing a team who were all five to ten years older than me, which I found challenging. I've also had bosses who are a lot older than me and their insecurities shocked me. These situations made me see that no one was feeling totally safe in their roles and I began to understand why there was tension. I found working in teams quite challenging, especially when you are essentially thrown in together, often at random. Another element of the multi-hyphen lifestyle is I get to pick a bespoke team; I get to work with a wider range of individuals from different companies and with different expertise; I get to work with people in other countries; and I get to cross-pollinate and brew ideas with people in co-working spaces.

Big-scale change is slow and the workplace is just one example of that. Changes need to be made in the working world on a micro level and this requires a big change in our overall mindset too. Asking for big or small changes to your role or working set-up is still met with a raised eyebrow, flexibility being one of the changes that is still treated as a massive perk rather than something that makes economic sense to a business. This quote from tech entrepreneur and co-founder of Amicable app Pip Wilson sums it up: 'I believe the opportunities for flexible – and effective – working that now exist for everyone are greater than they have ever been. But a societal mind-set change is imperative.'[5] If the number of new start-ups and multi-hyphenates keeps growing and the consistent rise in the gig economy continues, then it's increasingly important that we feel protected and we need more policies to make sure individual workers don't miss out on workplace benefits. It's a bigger conversation. It's a new system and structure that's needed, not just a quick tweak to the existing one.

Generational Myths

As George Orwell said: 'Each generation imagines itself to be more intelligent than the one that went before it, and wiser than the one that comes after it.'[6] We all think we are doing the right thing, but we have slightly different perspectives depending on a range of factors, such as the economy and the surroundings in which we grew up.

My grandfather owned a driving school in Exeter and just as he retired, people had started getting computers at work. He *just* missed the boat on having to turn things digital. And thank goodness! How BORING that would have been after decades of paperwork to have to painstakingly convert it all from hand-written files to then retire a few years later anyway. But the practicalities and efficiencies of digital is something we take very much for granted now. The idea of not having the Internet as an option feels totally alien to us but it's still relatively new in the grand scheme of things. We still haven't figured a lot of things out. We are all still in learning mode and always will be when it comes to tech. We are also a long way off becoming technology literate across generations when it comes to actually understanding how the tech we use is created, coded and brought to life. Multigenerational offices can be interesting to navigate when the younger generations don't place as much value on loyalty or hierarchy. The old system used to work. But a lot has changed in a very short space of time and while organisations pretend they are keeping up, they aren't.

It's time to bust the same old myths that are perpetuated. 'Our culture is currently obsessed with generational labels and the stereotypes that go with them,' says Jessica Kriegel, author of *Unfairly Labeled*. 'There's about 80 million Millennials right now and some of those Millennials are CEOs in Silicon Valley, and some of them are illegal immigrants in the Midwest who are waitressing somewhere,' Kriegel said. 'You really can't put them all in a box. And what we do is, we put them all in a box, and that box is really based on a middle-income, white, American person and then we just say that's the only kind of Millennial that exists right now.'[7] Jessica makes a good point on how we should look at individuals rather than just assuming what traits someone will have because of their generation:

'What really determines whether someone is frugal or if they want to save the world has to do with, did your parents feed you? Did you have an aunt that spoiled you? Did you have books in your home? Did you go to a good school?' she says. 'There are a million factors that go into determining the kind of person you are when you grow up, and this arbitrary 20-year-long age bracket that is widely accepted is not one of them.'[8] We can't deny that there are bigger factors at play than just the year you were born. According to the Recruitment and Employment Confederation (REC) we are going to see big changes as the 'Baby Boomers decline as a percentage of the workforce offset by the growing influence of younger generations who place a higher value on flexibility, work-life balance and personal development.'[9] If these values really do matter to the younger generation, which the studies say they do, then we can expect the workplace to move quite quickly over the next decade.

Perhaps the generational divide is most prominently shown by the labels used by older generations for young people, like 'lazy' or 'entitled' for millennials, for example. Really the gap in understanding is caused by a breakdown in communication about wants, needs and values in the workplace. Millennials often come up in the media as being 'work-shy' or 'snowflakes', which I don't think is a fair representation, they just want to live their lives differently because they know what's possible. Millennials who don't work full-time are part of the reason the NHS has staffing problems, according to Ian Cumming, chief executive of Health Education England quoted in *The Times*, 'the NHS would have to adapt to millennial preferences if it wanted to attract and keep young people.'[10] Millennial preferences mean flexibility and more choice over when to work. There have also been articles on American news sites of staffing shortages in both the police force and fire department because, reportedly, millennials either want too much flexibility or they are hopping from job to job too often. However, we can't blame a whole generation for behavioural changes or a changing mindset when it comes to work. The system around it is in need of changing too. The question should be: how do we cater to an increasingly flexible workforce across ALL industries? We have the chance to recalibrate what a working day looks like in industries across the world and how technology and automation can contribute in a positive way.

It is a myth that boomers aren't good with technology, just as much as it is a myth that all Gen Z youngsters are vacuous and totally obsessed with taking selfies. It doesn't make sense to broadly group people together that easily just because of the year you were born. Baby boomers are often thought of as not being digitally savvy but it's of course not always the case. According to a report by Google, baby boomers spend more time online than they do watching TV! They are more likely to share something on Facebook over and above younger generations. They've even been dubbed silver surfers. Boomers also have the most disposable income and most of the property ownership, so this is a generation who can afford to upgrade their homes with the latest gadgets. When it comes to leading a multi-hyphenate working lifestyle, it is definitely not suited to any one generation. Each generation benefits from flexibility, freedom and finding new skills.

In studies as early as 2010, Nielsen released reports showing that boomers spend the most money on tech: 'It's actually a myth that baby boomers aren't into technology. They represent 25% of the population, but they consume 40% [in total dollars spent] of it,' said Patricia McDonough, senior VP-analysis at Nielsen Co.[11] They also spend way more on online shopping than other generations on average according to Forrester Research's annual benchmark tech study. The future of work affects all generations, and all generations are able to reap the rewards of how the Internet can offer flexibility and new job roles or side-hustles. It would be unfair to think we are that different in how quickly we have adapted.

Social-media use in the older generations is on the rise too. According to the Office for National Statistics, one in four over-sixty-fives are now using social-networking sites such as Facebook and Twitter. Dubbed the 'Instagrans', the proportion of over-sixty-fives who say they are active on social sites grew by more than 50 per cent last year.[12]

The number of over-seventy-fives using social media has nearly doubled in the last year, Ofcom has found, with over 41 per cent of over-seventy-fives using it, up from 19 per cent the previous year.[13] Boomers enjoy growing their social-media followers and upgrading their tech as much as Gen Z.

Tim Kellett, director at Paydata (a management consultancy), says all employees with diverse skills should be seen as an asset to their employer. 'Employees are taking control of where and how they want to work, therefore employers need to be adaptable in order to retain such talent.'[14] Instead of just pushing millennials and Gen Z aside as being entitled, it might just mean that employers need to adjust the workplace in order to keep the talent within the organisation. Otherwise employees will leave and start their own project or company, because they can. As *Atlantic* writer Jean M. Twenge in her piece 'Have Smartphones Destroyed A Generation?' says: 'The aim of generational study, however, is not to succumb to nostalgia for the way things used to be; it's to understand how they are now.'[15] This is the main thing: we have to look forward, accept the reality of now. There's no point in being nostalgic for the old times unless there is a lesson or solution in it that we can apply to a new situation.

Where Are We Now?

When it comes to any sort of change, it's hard to write about it when we're still in the thick of it. It's hard to see any perspective because it's all around us, always changing and bending, like a kaleidoscope. But when it comes to the last few years, it feels like there have been dramatic shifts in how we make up our minds and how we express ourselves. The Internet has changed what we see. It's hard to tell if we know too much, with everything at our fingertips, or if we know nothing at all. When it comes to trust, skills, connection and culture, this has all changed since we've become so entrenched in our online worlds.

THERE'S BEEN A CHANGE IN TRUST

We have trust issues. Not me, or you, necessarily, but the world right now. The trust when it comes to leaders and people in political power is fragile and weak. The Internet is full of information we think twice about retweeting because we question whether it's true. The Edelman Trust Barometer is really interesting. It gives an indication on who trusts whom each year when it comes to the media, government, etc. I remember when the trust back in the earlier noughties had shifted from 'trusting the media' to 'trusting people like yourself' and people started trusting blog recommendations over TV adverts. Makes sense. But since then, the trust conversation has changed again. The 2017 Edelman Barometer revealed the largest ever drop in trust across government, business, media and NGOs. Trust in media fell and is at all-time lows in seventeen countries, while trust levels in government dropped in fourteen markets. The credibility of leaders also is in dire straits. CEO credibility dropped twelve points globally to an all-time low, plummeting in every country studied. Trust in authority is vanishing and is being replaced by trust in those closest to us and most like us. The UK population trusts their family and friends over four times more than political parties and leaders.[16] I don't think it's a coincidence that there's a lack of trust in public figures. Lies are often exposed online, more information is available to privately research and make sense of, and in America '88 percent of millennials saying they only "sometimes" or "never" trust the press.' I think this has a lot to do with the rise of anxiety. The less we trust our external sources, the more we worry. If we don't trust the grown-ups any more to sort things out, we take on that stress and anxiety in other areas of our lives. Without trust, everything can feel more up in the air and like it could collapse around us at any minute. Rebuilding trust, right now, is a matter of urgency.

THERE'S BEEN A CHANGE IN SKILLS NEEDED

I think a lot of crossed wires in the workplace are rooted in both misunderstanding and fear, and that fear is understandable. In a recent article Yuval Noah Harari said that 'by 2050 a new class of people might emerge – the useless class. People who are not just unemployed, but unemployable.'[17] Essentially he is saying that a lot of people will be pushed out of jobs because of robots and AI. He also says that very soon we will be in a situation where 'no one knows what to study at college, because no one knows what skills learned at 20 will be relevant at 40.' That is not a fun thing to hear, but feels very true. The challenge is to embrace these fears and create better working relationships. There's a line that Ta-Nehisi Coates said during a talk at the MacDowell Chairman's Evening where he spoke about his mentor David Carr, from the *New York Times*: 'He had this wonderful ability to not be afraid of young people. He would completely and totally invest in young people.' It made me realise just how many of my own bosses didn't necessarily try and lift the younger employees up or use the new skills available, instead they would often try and push them aside out of fear.

I grew up believing that if the Internet was going to be such a massive part of my life I had to also believe that I could make my life slightly easier because of it. The Internet has allowed me to shortcut my career. I have been able to give myself a platform in order to get more opportunities from many different corners. I've used Twitter to connect with employers, a blog to get more work and used the Internet in ways to hijack my own career and leapfrog my way into a hard-to-get-into industry. My full-time job in a corporate-marketing environment wasn't moving fast enough because the company was so big, so I experimented with new tools on the side. Just because your job doesn't offer you interesting, exciting ways to up your game or try things out, the good news is you can still do it in your spare time. I read up on things, curated Twitter lists, signed up to RSS feeds, launched websites, tested my Photoshop skills with free trials and realised that I didn't need to wait for some big company to train me, and even if they did it would be months or years too late. I had to train myself. And the best part was I could do it in thirty-minute chunks in the evenings or on Sunday mornings over a cup of coffee. I started to enjoy teaching myself new things, regularly, calmly and in my own time because it was never going to be wasted. The key is to stay curious and do it in manageable pieces of stolen time here and there.

Bruce Daisley from Twitter said something interesting in *The Times* about the slow-to-change nature of the modern workplace:

> If we had reflected 20 years ago about how the internet was going to change our jobs, the idea that you had to be at your desk at 9am and go home at 5.30pm was probably one of the first things we might have expected to go. But being at your desk is still considered one of our fundamental measures of whether people are doing a good job. We have not changed work, we have just put more stuff over the top.[18]

One reason the nine-to-five used to work for the Silent Gen was because at that time many people worked in a very physically demanding job where they were operating machinery by hand. It was also totally normal for one person to be the main breadwinner. One person (usually the man) used to go to work (and could work whatever hours, but usually nine-to-five) but it wouldn't matter because their spouse (usually the wife) could be at home and look after the kids. But we've moved on (thank God). But what happens when the two careers grow at the same speed? More flexibility and a more yin and yang approach is needed. There are so many new jobs that require part-time work or remote working that are suited to people who can't physically get into an office (new mums, carers, people with disabilities). This helps further workplace equality by creating more opportunities for all, regardless of personal matters.

THERE'S BEEN A CHANGE IN WHERE WE CAN WORK FROM

Not all jobs allow flexibility. But the nine-to-five genuinely baffled me, as someone who grew up learning basic coding skills, how to schedule content online while I'm sleeping and being able to multitask on my phone from age twelve. Millennials get given the label of 'entitled' but I don't mind taking one for the team. The notion of the nine-to-five working day was established in the Victorian era when no one really cared about the worker, so it's no surprise that it bewilders the modern generation. This is a generation who earn money from their bedrooms, because they want to (maybe) but also because they have to. It's confusing to have work emails on our phones while we're simultaneously told to work a rigid nine-to-five. I used to be that person answering my emails on the train into work, but if I was five minutes late, I would get death stares from all corners of the office.

In the 2001 book *The Body Clock Guide to Better Health* by Michael Smolensky and Lynne Lamber, the lark and owl theory (something I've always believed in) is explored. 'One in ten of us is an up-at-dawn, raring-to-go early bird, or lark. About two in ten are owls, who enjoy staying up long past midnight. The rest of us, those in the middle, whom we call hummingbirds, may be ready for action both early and late.'[19] It's therefore easy to understand where the nine-to-five has come from – factory and office workers needed light, shelter and face-to-face contact *and* the majority of people are hummingbirds. However, these differing body-clock types show that we don't all just fit neatly into one box or one period of time when we're at our best. Work flexibility should be more widespread, an hour moved here or there could have a massive positive change for some employees. We are so easily accessible now (perhaps too much so), so why not embrace it? I'm definitely an owl. The book says 'owls often skip breakfast, and they're always rushing to get to work in the morning.' Whereas give me a bit more time in the morning to get moving and I am an absolute winner at getting stuff done later in the day. We should be encouraged to figure these things out about ourselves early on at school. (That, and learning what taxes are.) Because your dream job could be dependent on your body clock: 'If you're a lark, you probably wouldn't enjoy a job as a nighttime bartender. If you're an owl, you'd have a struggle to report the morning news.'

In *Fast Company*, in an article entitled 'How To Design Your Ideal Workday Based on Your Sleep Habits', sleep expert Michael Breus said you could be a bear (average sleep pattern, 50–55 per cent of the population, with a morning routine of 7 a.m.–11 a.m.); a lion (wake up without alarm, around 15 per cent of the population, with a morning routine of 5.30 a.m.–10 a.m.); or a wolf (hate mornings, represent 15–20 per cent of the population with a morning routine of 7.30 a.m.–12 p.m.). With all this research into sleep patterns and productivity, why are we not embracing it more and using it to understand ourselves better and inform our workplace routine?

Flexibility is not just about digital millennial nomads with stickers on their MacBook Pros. We're talking single parents, people living in chronic pain, elderly workers and the list goes on. We could all benefit from having some more flex in our lives, and not feeling guilty about it either. Flexibility is also about productivity, because when the person is at the centre of their own schedule, they can get more done.

'The bottom line is that productivity—driven by technology and well-functioning markets—drives wealth far more than hours worked.' – a 2012 article for *Foreign Policy* by Charles Kenny.

THERE'S BEEN A CHANGE IN WORK CULTURE

Workplace culture is a funny one, isn't it? I've been told in many job interviews that my CV looks fine but what they really want to know is do I fit in with the culture of the office? What is workplace culture exactly? Essentially is it the character and personality of the organisation. It is the people, the community, the vibe and how you feel when you're there. The thing is, I've worked at companies where the culture was incredibly fun and motivating (Friday-afternoon group presentations! Free ski trips!), but I was miserable. I felt ungrateful. I felt privileged. But I also felt like the perks weren't making me happy at work, they were actually making me feel more attached to my day job, more indebted to the office, more guilty if I wanted any sort of flexibility outside of it. Successful workplace culture can't be just based on perks. Culture isn't just about free beers on a Friday. Culture isn't even free doughnuts. Culture goes so far beyond that. It's about how a place makes you feel and the people you work with.

I was interested in Twitter's new Culture 2.0 manifesto as an example of a company making change. In their New Work Manifesto there were many statements that resonated with me including '40 hours is enough', 'reclaim your lunch' and 'digital sabbath', inspiring employees to 'escape digital enslavement'. It is a sign that even digital-first companies are encouraging more offline time to bond with colleagues, be happier and more fulfilled. Work-life balance has never been so important, and not just for millennials.

A study in the US by *Fortune* found that on average, millennials would be willing to give up $7,600 in salary every year to work at a job that provided a better environment for them.[20] A sign that when it comes to working, our comfort and happiness in our surroundings matter and may even affect our decisions over which job to take. Our working environment is important and that spans across office culture, colleagues, flexibility allowance, natural lighting, up-to-date technology and what success looks like to the company.

THERE'S BEEN A CHANGE IN WORKPLACE HIERARCHY

A Deloitte study surveying more than seven thousand companies found that 92 per cent of those surveyed cited organisational redesign as 'the top priority'. Josh Bersin, who worked at

Deloitte on the study, suggested that people have less-defined jobs and move laterally from project to project.[21] In most modern-day jobs (although not all), hierarchy has had to take a back seat or at least been restructured or relooked at. Of course people who have been doing a job longer are by definition more experienced at that job (a surgeon, for example), but in the new roles that have only just been created we are seeing that a younger generation have self-taught, learned faster and there-fore have some niche knowledge at their fingertips. Climbing the ladder is not so simple any more. Hierarchies in the work-place used to be a successful way of getting workers to obey and follow the rules but that tactic won't work as well in the future.

Hierarchies don't work as well as they used to because expertise has changed. An expert doesn't necessarily look like a long-standing CEO, especially if they are removed from the day-to-day micro decisions. New industries and new ways of working are more likely to have niche experts who don't need decades of experience on their side to prove they are an expert. Expertise has nothing to do with age or amount of years spent in the field, you can become an expert by simply being in the deep end of it all. You can be an expert on the very thing you are creating as we are designing new jobs that haven't been done before. It's a great time to have a niche and own it. Broaden your horizons, add in different hyphens to your bio and capitalise on a time of huge change where a small idea can turn into something very big indeed. It is a time to not be intimidated by others, and work towards creating your own expertise.

A myth that comes with the multi-hyphenate tag is that having a diverse career must mean you cannot be an expert because you are a jack of all trades. But why does being an expert need to mean you can only have a career in one area? We can be an expert in a few things. Gone are the days where you dedicate your entire life to one thing. What's interesting about the workplace right now is that so many jobs are still evolving, there is a whole wealth of new industries, sectors and niches that don't have any experts yet and there are future jobs that don't yet exist. You can be an expert regardless of your age, for example, whereas before you would have to spend years and years on something and the only way to become an expert was learning from others. Tech has opened up so many more ways to become an expert, by simply doing, experimenting and teaching yourself. Now is the time to make your own expertise in a new area of your career. The democratisation of online education and tools means that anyone can get to an expertise level in a new area of tech without traditional training simply because when a course is created it cannot be up to date for more than a few months. By simply doing things enough times, you can pick up new skills. This is not about people being marginally good at a variety of things, it's about picking multiple skills to hone that complement each other. This book is about busting the myth that you can truly only be good at one thing. The idea that everyone must be an expert in one thing plays into this traditional idea of success and the idea that you must climb the same ladder as those before you. We're less enamoured by the vertical ascent of a shiny corporate ladder, we also want our own individual linear path that reflects our chosen lifestyle.

It's important that companies learn to move more quickly and become more nimble to change. In a piece by Aaron

Dignan, investor and founder of The Ready (a company that helps organisations redesign their structure) he said: 'Even in a self-organized, decentralized, collaborative, and high-trust future (in fact, especially in that future), people will need to navigate their organization. Data will need to flow transparently and fluidly across the network. Roles and projects will need to be created, filled, and disbanded with increasing frequency.'[22] This means that job titles potentially won't last as long. The company will be updating itself so often and remaining so agile that we won't have the choice to feel married to our job title or job identity. We will move with the changes and keep upgrading our positions naturally, depending on the work. This is another reason why a lot of people go it alone, start a side-project or invest in a project alongside their job because they can do it more quickly without the layers of approval that exist in some companies. They can learn, grow, take risks and experiment without needing sign-off from ten people every time. In some cases small projects leapfrog over big organisations and grow from scratch, for example a company like Airbnb overtaking and booking more rooms than the world's largest hotel chains.[23] Having a creative hyphen outside of your job can allow you to add and experiment with the fast-changing skills that will be needed in a bigger company (but a stagnating big company might not allow you to learn them quickly enough). Those skills can add to your job in many beneficial ways or your side-project could take on legs of its own. It's a win-win situation.

Be Inspired by the 'Yes, And . . .' Generation

When we think about teenagers now, in many ways they grow up more quickly – embracing technology, learning about things online, having Google at their fingertips for any questions they might have. This comes with its downsides of course but in many ways the Internet can be educational. Phillip Picardi, Chief Content Officer at *Teen Vogue*, said in an interview with Coveteur: 'Teens are very much the "Yes, And . . ." generation. They're always on top of new things before you are and you always have to keep that in mind.'[24] Scott Hess, a seeming multi-hyphenate himself, on LinkedIn it says 'Executive Vice President (Corporate Marketing, Generational Intelligence) also: poet' at Spark, a media agency said: 'These guys are actually together by voice on gaming networks, and visually on Skype or Google Chat as they do their homework together. It's still virtual interaction, but it's full sight, sound and motion rather than just texts.'[25] This adds to the reason this generation are full of ideas, always building on them and in constant connection.

Due to their own education and additional self-taught education growing up with tech, Gen Z know they can get more from their pay cheque so they expect it. Millennials were slightly different, they still followed in the old steps of the baby boomers – get a good education at school, degree, chasing a corporate job and getting on a ladder. Tech and social media hadn't blossomed yet – millennials didn't quite know what they could do with it or the extent of it. For example, huge YouTubers such as Zoella and Louise Pentland both felt vulnerable leaving their full-time jobs to go into the unknown at the time. Zoella famously says her dad told her to get a 'real job' at the beginning, because nothing had been proven yet. It hadn't been done before. Gen Z have seen these niche careers unfold and they have seen that good money can be made *and* that you can use a platform to make a difference. Millennials realised that something needed to change. The path the baby boomers took couldn't work in the same way for us, so perhaps this is why millennials rebranded the portfolio career (I've called it the Multi-Hyphen Method) – it's a way of getting out of a sticky career situation and resolving a problem, be it short term or long term. Whereas a lot of Gen Z creatives aren't even entertaining the corporate handshake, they're multi-hyphenates from the get-go. Fewer Gen Zers are going to university because of this change, too. According to Daria Taylor, co-founder of Talented Heads, a digital-marketing agency, 'We'll see more of this generation not going to university because of the high cost, but going straight into the workplace — and maybe doing some online studies.' It appears that Gen Z are going to go straight into the thick of it, because university courses could be out of date by the time they learn them and get into the working world and the Internet is there to allow them to present themselves. This means that a lot of Gen Z have to take their own risks, find their own path, they can't necessarily ask their parents for advice, much like millennials.

It's very easy to just brush young people aside as being narcissistic but it's unfair. It's unfair because this is the environment they have grown up in. It is an environment that rewards them for having likes on social media. But on the positive side it's an environment that always rewards people for putting yourself out there. If you don't foghorn about yourself or your achievements, who else will? As Phillip Picardi says: 'This is not just the selfie generation or selfish millennials, this is an audience who is uniquely engaged in changing the world by being involved in social justice.'

It feels like, on the whole, most of us do want to have some sort of impact. Social media, publishing, activism and building our own entrepreneurial empires online come from a place of caring about the future. Because the gatekeepers have changed, and in some cases crumbled, we don't need a traditional publishing deal to have our voices heard. A quote from Seth Godin on the popular Tim Ferriss podcast spoke to me recently. He said:

> Social media wasn't invented to make you better. It was invented to make the companies money. And you are an employee of the company and you are the product that they sell. And they have put you in a little hamster wheel and they throw little treats in now and then. But you gotta decide, what's the impact you're trying to make?

If social media is just a hamster wheel and we are making Internet companies money, then it makes sense to try and have some impact along the way. Impact on our own lives, impact on our friends' lives and even impact on the world around us. Finding out who we are matters. Having a strong sense of self matters. Having a purpose matters. Don't be afraid to have multiple careers and interests.

What Actually Motivates Us?

So, reflecting on this change in culture, skills and trust over the years, what actually motivates us? It's interesting that a big part of our lives now does not feature on Abraham Maslow's (an American psychologist) hierarchy of needs pyramid. Maslow's 'A Theory of Human Motivation', which he put down on paper in 1943, stated that humans had physiological needs (air, food, shelter, sex, sleep), safety needs (security, law, order), love needs (friendship, family, trust, love), esteem needs (dignity, independence, respect from others) and finally self-actualisation needs (seeking personal potential and growth). We live in a privileged society now where we can spend more time on our self-growth, rather than just basic primitive survival. Maslow's pyramid was created in a time when 80 per cent of workers still worked in a factory.[26] It seems as though Wi-Fi and social media would definitely be added on to this pyramid if it was reimagined nowadays.

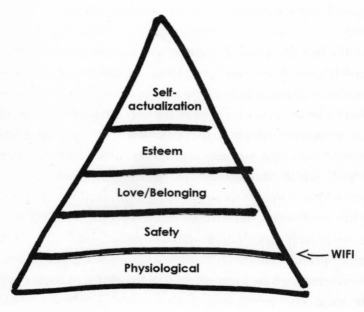

Millennials have become the group in society that people gently mock for being good with the Internet, but assume are really bad at holding down a job. Really, all they are doing is rebelling against the status quo of the traditional office. But there's a much deeper reason behind not being able to commit to one job and it's nothing to do with the fear of hard work. It's to do with the fact that the world is currently changing at breakneck speed. Millennials are adapting and taking advantage of their niche set of skills. Maybe the confidence in taking risks in their working lives is because they perhaps don't have any big material items to lose so it's worth trying. For example, millennials have taken on at least 300 per cent more student debt than their parents,[27] so they are already on the back foot financially and they are less likely to own property and more likely to have kids later, so why not have a side-hustle too, that they will enjoy and can bring in some extra cash?

What is classed as traditional work has drastically changed over the last few years. My job as social-media editor did not properly exist five years ago. I was told off for going on to Myspace at school when, just like many others, I was teaching myself how to code for the first time. Coding was one of the most in-demand jobs of 2015. Even since 2010, social-media positions were up 1,357 per cent on LinkedIn.[28] Statistics from the BBC World Service say that '65% of jobs haven't been invented yet.'[29] We are in a state of industry flux. We are learning the art of selling ourselves and our skills online by connecting with employers online, boosting our personal search-engine optimisation (SEO) and doing things that will make our online presence look impressive. In 2008, there were zero big-data architects (people trained to describe the structure and behaviour of big data) on LinkedIn. In 2013, there were 3,440. (It might not come as a shock that nearly 70 per cent of parents admit they don't have a clear understanding of their children's jobs).[30] The motivation behind the work choices of millennials is very much dependent on the jobs they are naturally good at and drawn to (due to our initiation period of the online world, having grown up online) and what is available to them.

According to a new study from Elance, 87 per cent of the UK's top-performing graduates see freelancing as a highly attractive career option. In the US, Bentley University researched how equipped graduates were for the workplace. Two-thirds of interviewees planned to launch companies, while 37 per cent wanted to work alone.[31] The death of the nine-to-five is on the rise with millennials more likely to gig instead of sticking to one company. Employers could benefit from this by hiring per project, by person, by expertise to get the most concentrated quality of work at all times.

And what do Gen Z expect from the workplace? According to data by Randstad, Gen Z are 5 per cent more likely than millennials to work for themselves (millennials 32 per cent and Gen Z 37 per cent).[32] Money may have also a different meaning to Gen Z, 46 per cent of whom say that their biggest financial concern is student debt, which has increased year on year in the UK, and America especially. Gen Z also not only want employers to allow them on social media and advanced tech, many of them are increasingly interested in integrating emerging technologies, such as wearables, virtual reality and robotics, into the workplace. It is also interesting that 45 per cent of digital-native generations want to have a career in technology, a number that continues to grow. For many people, especially the younger gens getting started, it's almost useless thinking of the profession you want to go into. According to Jean-Philippe Michel, an Ottawa-based career coach, there's no such thing as a profession now: 'They need to shift from thinking about jobs and careers to think about challenges and problems.'[33] He believes, like me, that we need to 'prepare the next generation for a career in the future, which for many will be made up of numerous micro-jobs aimed at well-paid skilled workers, and not a single boss and company.' New companies, like The Hoxby Collective, provide services to business by handpicking 'a team of specialists from around the world specifically for your brief; bringing together only the finest talent, only when you need it.' YunoJuno is a company that connects experts and multi-hyphenates to the job or micro-job remotely. The Dots, founded by Pip Jamieson, which has been called 'the Linkedin for creatives' by Techcrunch, is a network that connects freelancers in fashion, the arts and technology to new clients and has recently raised £4million in funding. These sorts of companies and services will be on the rise, allowing us to work in a way that suits us and that gets the job done productively, with the business on the other side really benefiting from getting the best, most talented experts for the job.

This is miles away from the old metric of working hard, which used to be face-time at a desk and how obedient you were to the system. Millennials are working smarter and harder than ever by juggling multiple projects all from their one Wi-Fi connection.

But it's not just millennials that are constantly evolving along with an ever-changing digital world and seeing themselves as brands, not just employee #105, we are all waking up to the future. Instead of believing we are just another faceless cog turning in a company, we are all starting to build a USP. Whether that's our personal Instagram page, designing digital identities, growing communities, launching campaigns or starting businesses. Working hard has taken on a whole new meaning and some of it is invisible to the outside world.

Even Pharrell Williams has been sticking up for millennials recently (they need it):

'Millennials are socialists and nobody has noticed. They're not interested in owning a house, they Airbnb. They don't need to own a super-fast car, they get in a Lyft or an Uber. They're about being communal. So all those old people that are up there'— he gestures somewhere in the metaphorical direction of the White House—'fighting for everything, trying to keep everything closed off, partitions everywhere: it's OK 'cos you're old. And at the end of the day, these kids are the future. I'm old, too!'[34]

The bit that stuck out for me the most here was when Pharrell made a point about generations outgrowing themselves and needing to make room for other generations coming up below them. This makes the obvious but important point that nothing is permanent. We are constantly changing and growing, and one day Gen Z will be the biggest proportion of the workforce and the key decision-makers, so we have no choice but to be open-minded about the future.

Today, driven by tremendous transparency in the job market, we change jobs often. And it's across all generations now. The average baby boomer will be looking for a job 11.7 times in his or her career, according to a Bureau of Labor Statistics study, and millennials change jobs every two years or less.[35] Olivia Gagan wrote an interesting piece for Refinery29 on the reality of millennials and why they are turning to creating so much online: 'While home ownership was an achievable reality for our parents and grandparents, it's now just a fantasy for millions of millennials, and people are making TV, theatre, music and poetry about it.'[36]

According to a study by HSBC, 89 per cent of people surveyed by the bank (of all ages) said the thing that would motivate them to be most productive at work is flexibility. This was then followed by remote working and then (lower on the list) things like a bonus scheme, learning courses, extra sick days and healthcare insurance.

We are all evolving and adopting faster than we think. We can't make judgements or put any one generation into one stereotyped category. It's time we made sure the imaginary barriers don't get in the way of working together, especially when it comes to the future of work. The media love to spin a sensational headline about millennials vs other generations but perhaps we are much more similar than we think.

Practical Exercises

What about you? What motivates you? What makes you excited to wake up? What is it that drives your hunger and ambition? Only when you know and understand your key motivations can you work back in order to create your own definition of success.

Some days go by in a whirlwind and I don't get the chance to understand why *on that day* I felt motivated. But what I try to do is make a list of the smaller moments when I'm feeling motivated and then try to unpick them and understand them by asking questions such as:

1. Was my personal life affecting anything?
2. Do I respond better to certain environments?
3. What sort of people motivate me?
4. What sort of people drain me?
5. Are there days I enjoy more than others?
6. Do some days feel easier than others? Why?
7. What days excite me the most?

Try this exercise yourself.

With the responses to these questions, what answers are you left with? Visualise all of your answers by drawing your own spider diagram, just like my one on the previous page.

CHAPTER 3

The Rise of the Multi-Hyphenate

'You are not only one person! But dozens, hundreds of personalities! But boy you might never meet all of them! We try so hard to fit into boxes, that we end up suppressing some of what we are and end up living the wrong lives.' – Freddie Harrel, fashion entrepreneur[1]

You now understand that the Multi-Hyphen Method is a lifestyle approach to embracing your own definition of success, having different projects and income streams coming in at the same time. It is essentially about being a happier person at work, but it also has economic business sense behind it. It's about breaking out of a predetermined definition of success that's been passed down to you or has seeped into your mind subconsciously through external sources. But it also doesn't necessarily mean leaving a day job. This isn't a 'quit your job'-type book. It's also not about labelling yourself a 'freelancer'. It could be that you have an outside-of-work hobby – or hyphen – adding to what you do. A side-project doesn't have to mean world domination or a global business plan, but it does mean making time for more self-care, or building and enjoying learning new skills on the side. It is the straight-up refusal to be pigeonholed in the modern working world and not being afraid to add another strand to your career bio. It is rebelling against being a) defined by what generation you fall into and b) mindlessly following someone else's path. You are not your job title, instead you move in between different jobs, alongside powerful strategic personal branding, you funnel, organise, outreach, monetise and schedule your work yourself.

This is not about having fifteen jobs that you don't like and juggling to make ends meet, tearing your hair out at night. This is an active choice to have more than one job, a career with multiple strands that suits you. The Multi-Hyphen Method is about having fingers in pies, yes, but it's about picking and choosing the projects you work on in a very strategic way and building your personal brand along the way.

We shouldn't assume that freelance flexibility and multiple career strands means 'gigging'. Gigging has negative connotations, sometimes described as a specific type of exploitation with inconsistent hours and bad communication. Flexibility is a far more nuanced option than the full-time nine-to-five and unsupported gigging. There is a vast and varied spectrum of options in between these two extremes. According to the Office for National Statistics, at the beginning of 2016 the self-employed accounted for 15 per cent of the UK population. That's 4.6 million people. That's a lot of people who could do with more advice, tools, resources, direction and opportunities for work. Work hasn't moved on fast enough so right now it's up to us to explore the options and advantages. This is about harnessing multiple skills and housing them under one career roof.

THE MULTI-HYPHENATE LIFESTYLE IS ABOUT . . .
* allowing yourself space to breathe
* allowing yourself to not be defined by a box that having one job – with a title chosen by someone else – can put you in
* having the courage and tools to make big moves on the side, without risking financial stability
* giving yourself the confidence to not be defined by one thing
* letting go of thinking your job is your life, your identity and your worth
* letting yourself add other names and titles to your bio as you go
* letting your hobbies and joyful moments make you better at your job
* having two simultaneous careers, or more, whatever ratio works for you
* allowing technology to help you live a happier, more creative lifestyle
* getting rid of the labels put on us by work traditions of the past
* unchaining yourself from a system that loves to box us in and make us feel trapped for life

Your hyphens don't even have to be work-related to make a difference. Your hyphen could be 'parent' or 'carer' or 'poker champion' or 'chief knitter' or 'flash mobber'. It doesn't need to be a side-hustle or hyphen that makes you money. It can work as an enjoyable bonus and outlet alongside your job. Of course additional income is amazing and can be a by-product of having multiple projects, cash flow can increase in abundance. But it all starts with incentive, intention, enjoyment and curiosity. This is all about having a mix that works for you. It's about owning your own combinations of full-time, part-time and flexible working. This is a new age of employment. You are running your own business, with a mixture of skills to offer. It's about creating and maintaining security and your own online ecosystem.

FOUR MYTH-BUSTERS – YOU CAN BE A
MULTI-HYPHENATE *AND* . . .

- have totally different interdisciplinary careers. They can often look totally different on the surface but complement each other in interesting ways
- still be an expert in one or more areas even if you have multiple interests or hyphens to your job title
- not be overly ambitious! Having a multi-hyphenate career isn't always about being the best, or being the hardest hustler. But it is about having a cocktail of projects and work that makes you feel satisfied and driven
- still maintain a successful day job or part-time job, with added career strands added on the side. The beauty of this lifestyle is you don't have to pick just one way of working.

It's Time to be Unapologetic

I used to apologise for everything, I would just be sorry all the time. I would apologise if *someone else* spilled their coffee on me. I would apologise for taking up any space, breathing air. Another thing I would always apologise for were my lifestyle and career choices. For years I have apologised for how I work and when I work. I used to go home and run my side-projects in the evenings and was met with judgement from colleagues and acquaintances, perhaps because I looked like I was a crazy person, trying to build a moonlight side business on no sleep. I asked my employer if I could have Wednesday afternoons off so that I could finish writing my first book. It felt rebellious as it wasn't really the norm. I'd leave the office on Wednesday at 1 p.m., by the time I got home it would be 2 p.m. and I'd write from then until 6 p.m. Four solid hours of side-hustle time. But before leaving the office every week I would apologise, feel guilty, make an awkward joke and sidle out while everyone else was tapping away. The thing is, I'd asked and I'd got the flexibility I wanted. So why did it feel like I was committing a weird crime? Why did I feel like some of my other colleagues were side-eyeing me? Why did I feel guilty that I had flexibility at work, but I wasn't a parent? I wanted four hours a week to dedicate to my side-project, the side-project that ended up sparking my career trajectory and it was adding nicely to my finances.

Sometimes we have to take risks and be unapologetic for the things we want. It can feel awkward at the time, but later down the line you'll be so glad you pushed through. Do you have something you wish you had more time to do? Even the smallest amount of time to see if it's feasible? Do you think it's time to ask your employer for the flexibility to try it out?

In June 2016, I was selected to feature in a national TV advert with Microsoft. It played in cinemas and in the breaks of shows like *Britain's Got Talent*. In the thirty-second clip, I say 'Millennials will have more than five jobs in their lifetime and I think it's very exciting.' This sentence was born out of the Chase Jarvis quote: 'If our parents had one job, we'll have five, and the next generation will have five at the same time.'[2] A proportion of people perhaps didn't get it. How can you get a whole premise across or discuss any element of the future of work in just thirty seconds? I love the advert, but I knew I wanted to discuss this in more detail. The reason I said it was exciting is because it means we are going to be less boxed in as we grow and evolve and switch up our jobs.

I was selected to feature in this advert because I was a technology-obsessed and self-defined multi-hyphenate in the workplace. I have always been someone who could never put herself in a box and for years this made me feel insecure. But when a huge technology brand wanted to showcase my career story on a national platform (TV, cinemas, all over the Internet) perhaps it was the confirmation I needed to prove that this way of working is something to be taken seriously. I'd had no prior confirmation, only people raising their eyebrows and wondering why I didn't want to have a safe monthly salary.

This idea of what is now safe is interesting to me in this changing world of work. Can one job really be that safe anyway right now? Because I think what we thought *was* safe and what *is* actually safe is different, or at least is changing. The job-for-life scenario with a great deal of safety and pension security that we saw our parents and grandparents have no longer exists for us. But we all want security and deserve to feel secure in our jobs. People seem to ask me these questions a lot: Don't you feel unstable? Don't you miss your monthly salary? My answers: One, I felt more unstable working for a company that I didn't believe could transform itself enough to get through the technology revolution (I thought some of my old workplaces would fold and some actually did). And two, I do make a salary, just in a different, pieced-together sort of way.

I feel *much* more secure and confident knowing that by having multiple skills I have a diverse digital CV and I'm more employable. In the documentary *The Future Of Work And Death* it points out that 'one of things that has been born out of technological revolution is the ability to replace workers with more efficient machines.'[3] The process in general is called automation and lots of jobs could be replaced by machines. The future looks unpredictable, so how can we pretend that sitting at a nine-to-five desk is stable or secure?

We are all entrepreneurs now. The very meaning and idea of what an entrepreneur is has changed (it's not just people in Silicon Valley, it's you, it's me, it's anyone sat at their kitchen table with an idea) and the playing field has been levelled. In my head the idea of an entrepreneur was always someone in a suit, pitching in a board meeting. Rid yourself of the idea of what an entrepreneur looks or sounds like. Get rid of the stereotypes that the media peddle in terms of what a successful businessperson looks like. Those old ideas are fading fast. If you have a smartphone or a laptop and an idea, you can be entrepreneurial. You can start an online marketplace, launch an Instagram page, sell tickets, make a podcast or grow an attractive online portfolio. As Muhammad

Yunus, Nobel Peace Prize winner and microfinance pioneer, pointed out: 'All human beings are entrepreneurs. When we were in the caves, we were all self-employed . . . finding our food, feeding ourselves. That's where human history began. As civilization came, we suppressed it. We became "labor" because they stamped us, "You are labor." We forgot that we are entrepreneurs.'[4]

We are told that some of us have an entrepreneurial mindset and some of us don't, but I don't believe that. Just as I don't believe that only some of us are creative. We are all creative. We are all entrepreneurial. It's just whether you want to put it into practice or not.

The Multi-Hyphen Method is about giving you the confidence to branch out, try new things, grow your own portfolio, launch a new business, refuse to be labelled for life, own the fact that you don't have one thing you're good at. It's okay to have different things going on. The common denominator is you. You are the person who stitches it all together. You are the glue that holds together a bullet-point list of interests and career choices. Juggle, grow, explore, then whatever happens to our working world or whatever technology is next invented or whatever the new trends are, you will have everything you need to adapt and pivot. This is about giving yourself the permission to have more control of your choices and future.

It's Time to Start a Side-Hustle – for Your Bank Account or Just for Yourself

A side-hustle has been described as 'a low-risk project, meaning it shouldn't take a lot of start-up capital.'[5] That might sound a bit too 'business speak' but essentially it's something that encourages you to learn new skills or enjoy a passion project that doesn't take a lot of upfront investment in time or money. It isn't strictly work or play, but something in between. It's important that we all learn more about the tech we use and keep an eye on what is being said about the future of tech so that we don't end up with a huge imbalance of skills. Tech is already quite unequal when it comes to who is the most skilled in it. Tech itself is a feminist issue. Caitlin Moran commented, 'If you look at the stats on coding, it's still crackers isn't it?' (The latest research says 92 per cent of software engineers are men.)[6] 'That's like if the global language was going to be Chinese, and women weren't learning Chinese. The future is tech, the future is coding, this is how we build the world, this is how we understand ourselves.'[7]

Side-hustling is not just a trendy turn of phrase, it is a genuine add-on to many workers' lifestyles in the UK. According to research by GoDaddy, 48 per cent of those who start up a side-business do so to make money from a passion or a hobby, with some entrepreneurs reportedly earning between £500 and £5,000 on top of the salary from their day job.[8] According to data by Bankrate, one in four millennials have a side-hustle or different hyphens to their work. Sixty-one per cent of millennials working a side-hustle are at it once a week or more, 96 per cent are at their side-hustle at least once a month and 25 per cent say their side-hustle earns them $500 a month or more.[9]

It's clear we want to shake things up a bit. As many as 81 per cent of traditional workers (in America) surveyed said they would 'be willing to do additional work outside of [their] primary job if it was available and enabled [them] to make more money.'[10] That's a huge number of people who would be willing to have multiple jobs, but remember the aim is to not do it and burn out. The Multi-Hyphen Method is about having *more* flexibility, *more* freedom but *less* actual working hours.

There are reasons to start very small with a side-hustle as you can see how it is received initially and how much it might be worth growing. By launching a side-hustle using a small amount of your time (like one hour a week) you can see how viable it is, put your creative energy into something outside of your day job, experiment with ways you could monetise it and even if it is a tiny amount of money at the start, you are less stressed about it *having* to be a success. Using your time wisely means you can grow things on the side without risking your employment.

My first side-hustle came about because I hated my job. I was miserable. The work culture was toxic, disguised by perks which only made you feel like you had to stay longer at work, and the back-stabbing and competitive environment led me to get ill. My boyfriend reminded me that I cried literally all the time (I think I've blocked out those memories). I got cystitis from sitting at my desk and being too afraid to nip to the toilet in between conference calls (I wouldn't wish cystitis on my worst enemy).

So my saviour, my only saviour during these low moments at work, was going home and working on a project that I could do on my laptop, in the TV ad breaks or in my bedroom. It was heaven to be able to explore something different and work on a fun hustle. A side-hustle for me was something I enjoyed doing anyway, but I could faintly see a glimpse of opportunity in the future if I carried on doing it. Side-hustles don't have to be financially orientated, in fact it's better if they're not. That's why they are called side-hustles, because your main hustle is what pays you for the most hours in the day. An article in Quartz said that 'Millennials didn't invent the second job, they just branded it.'[11] People have always had multiple jobs, but the millennial generation, who are mostly told 'You can be whatever you want to be!' are freaked out by the hierarchy and the slow pace of the workplace and are using side-hustles to get ahead.

A see-saw side-hustle is something that allows you to stop and start a particular project. It doesn't take up all your time and it can be resurrected as and when you need it. You might want to have a bunch of side-projects that can ebb and flow depending on how much work they are accumulating and how much time you have to give to them at a particular time of year.

PROS for undertaking the Multi-Hyphen Method

- Variety makes us happier and less bored. We are all more multifaceted than we think.

- Intense periods of energy on projects results in higher-quality work. It is exciting to work on something and give it everything you have with an end date in mind.

- Your overall brand of you is the umbrella for your multiple projects.

An investment in your personal brand will make you stand out in the workplace.

- Productivity levels increase when you have some element of say on when you work, depending on your body clock, energy cycles and personal situation.

- You can earn more money in a concentrated time period.

- It enables you to move on from having one career and instead create an overall lifestyle that's unique to you and that you can control.

- You can embrace the idea of a non-linear career (aka not climbing a pre-made ladder created by someone else).

- You are not labelled. You are not boxed in. You are not defined by one career.

- You are open to exploring your potential in multiple areas.

- You are more employable in future years because you have a variety of skills. You cannot be phased out. You are adaptable.

- You are future-proofing yourself. You are learning to twist and turn as you go.

- You can move quickly. In a big corporation something as simple as designing a logo can take weeks, when you're a small business or by yourself it can be done in a matter of hours. Getting time back is important and being nimble is one of the most important things companies need to focus on right now.

CONS of undertaking the Multi-Hyphen Method

- It's a ball-ache describing what you do to your grandparents.

- You have to set some serious boundaries. Work-life blend only works when you have some parameters in place.

- The character limit in your Twitter bio isn't enough to sum it all up.

- People will want to put you into a box because it might make them uncomfortable that you don't have one clear job.

- You have to motivate yourself, which at times, can be difficult to sustain.

Real-life Multi-Hyphenates

Twelve case studies from a variety of different industries and career mixes. Here's how they make it work in individual ways.

TILLY, WORKS IN A PUB – FREELANCE FILM WORK

'Having multiple jobs definitely makes me feel like I'm using my time more wisely, allowing myself multiple avenues in my life, both personally and professionally. It gives me a real feeling of accomplishment, like I'm pushing myself to achieve more, even just day-to-day. My ability to work under pressure is utilised in both jobs, as are my communication skills and many other things, and so each job aiding my performance in the other also makes me feel fulfilled.'

OLIVIA, FREELANCE COPYWRITER – CONTENT DESIGNER – PERSONAL TRAINER

'I have this work set-up by choice, after years of realising what gets me up in the morning, what I'm good at and what pays the bills. While I feel like I am making a positive impact through the power of my laptop – helping organisations who do some incredible things – the type of interaction from personal training is much more immediate and instantly gratifying. Switching between an email-centric, meeting-friendly freelancer to instructing a fitness class or a PT session challenges me to utilise both my personas on a regular basis. It means I don't get too complacent doing one thing for a long period of time.'

HARRIET, FOUNDER OF ONLINE GIFT-BOX BROWNIE COMPANY NUTKINS BAKERY – SENIOR PR CONSULTANT – VIRTUAL ASSISTANT FOR A SMALL YOGA COMPANY

'I tend to do 75 per cent for Nutkins Bakery, which consists of baking, packaging orders, posting them out, business admin, marketing and PR. I then spend about 25 per cent of my day doing freelance work, whether it's PR projects or as a virtual assistant answering emails and creating social content for a small yoga brand. It can be tiring spinning multiple plates, but most days I work from home so it's much easier. One thing I would say is that organisation is key. I plan out my week on a Sunday and I always try to block out chunks of time for each project – without my bullet journal I wouldn't know if I was coming or going. Having such different jobs certainly makes me feel creatively fulfilled and it's also empowering knowing that I have control over the projects I'm working on and the type of work I'm accepting. It makes me feel much more in control and independent than I did when I worked in the corporate world. I love that I can create my own days on my own time schedule and if I need to change things around, I can. I quit my nine-to-five to have more freedom and to pursue a personal passion – having my fingers in multiple pies has allowed me to do that while also earning a living.'

EMMA, SENIOR PAEDIATRIC CLINICAL RESEARCH NURSE AT A CHILDREN'S HOSPITAL – A WRITER WITH A TWO-BOOK DEAL

'I feel lucky to have opportunities in both nursing and writing and I am pleased to be putting my education in both areas to good use. My job as a research nurse for children with rare diseases is fulfilling in the sense that I feel part of the driving force of change and innovation for treatment and medication. I also feel a sense of achievement as a soon-to-be published author. I like working in a clinical environment and having patient contact and then spending the evening in the company of publishers and writers and having entirely different experiences within a single day.'

JAYNE, CREATIVE DIRECTOR – WRITER – SOCIAL-MEDIA MANAGER – PHOTO EDITOR – ILLUSTRATOR[12]

'I've always been creative and I've always promoted my work on the Internet, so I feel like I'm coming to a natural balance of roles now. I also like to have variety in my day so these multiple job descriptions allow me to work on a mixture of projects, which keeps things interesting. This mixture of tasks keeps me fulfilled. I still don't know what the end result of my career will be in five, ten + years, but right now I like to be flexible with this as you never know what opportunities might turn up in the future or what skills you might pick up and adore along the way.'

ALEXA, WORKS AT FACEBOOK – SINGER – FOUNDED HER OWN COMPANY #ENTRYLEVELBOSS

'I work normal hours at Facebook, from roughly 10 a.m.–6 p.m. Every once in a while, I might dip out on a lunch break to work on something or take a call. As for EntryLevelBoss and music: I'm really productive on weekday nights and during the day on weekends. On the whole, I believe that my particular brand of magic comes from deconstructing career fairy tales and, instead, teaching people how to achieve things their way. And that starts by being open with the people who follow along with my career. I've never identified with the term "side-project". At the end of the day, it's all me. It's all connected.'

ALI, PRODUCT CONSULTANT WITHIN THE HR INDUSTRY – CHILDREN'S WRITER

'I prioritise my consultancy work in terms of when I work. I usually agree working days for the month and let the team know when I'm in the London office and when I'll be available but working remotely. If there's a need for me to be in the office on different days I swap them around or do additional hours. The remainder of the week is managing the small design and development team I've brought together. Being able to swap heads, although a bit hectic and stressful at times, enables me to get much rounder job satisfaction.'

ALLY, PARAMEDIC – BLOGGER – PHOTOGRAPHER

'I'm currently working full-time with the ambulance service so that takes up most of my time because I've been doing a lot of training, but will be back to my normal schedule in the next few weeks which means regular blocks of days off to fit in photography and blogging. On the occasions where the one job has taken over entirely I've felt . . . well . . . unfulfilled is the perfect word for it. Eventually I'd like to go part-time with the ambulance service and spend more time on my photography and blogging. But regardless I'd still want to carry on with all three.'

VICTORIA, TRAINEE SOLICITOR – CEO OF BIG VOICE LONDON, A SOCIAL-MOBILITY CHARITY

'I've always been the sort of person that prefers to be busy, so having multiple roles suits me well. Working in two different

industries, particularly where they are slightly interconnected, is also a bonus. I know that I'm making the most of
my time and my skills – both roles challenge me in different
ways. I'm constantly learning during my training as a solici-
tor, I'm improving my legal advice, my approach to litigation
and my drafting. With my work at Big Voice London, I'm
learning how to grow a charity, building relationships with
sponsors and leading a team of people. I have no doubt that
doing both roles simultaneously is making me better at both
jobs as a result.'

ADAM, PODCAST PRODUCER – CHEF

'I was originally just a chef, but podcast production grew and
grew. I began with one show and now produce two. I literally
finish at the restaurant and go to work straight away on the
podcasts. It was a choice, as I could have scaled back my
podcasting ambitions, but now that I earn almost half my
income from podcasting, I hope to grow it further, and so am
pouring my efforts into it. I always struggled to find the right
creative outlet and for many years felt that I was merely existing to work. However, now that I have this creative outlet, I do
feel as though I am achieving more with my life.'

LOUISE, YOGA TEACHER – LIFE COACH – PHD – NURSE

'I am in charge of my own schedule. I can choose whatever
days I want off and when to go on holidays. My PhD and life-
coaching business and additionally writing my book mean I
can work from anywhere. Currently my regular weekly yoga
classes and the odd nursing shifts I do keep me in London but
I could easily move and work abroad tomorrow if I wanted to.

The idea that my earning potential is limitless is also another huge plus.'

DONNA, MARKETING CONSULTANT –
COACH – EVENT ORGANISER

'I try to book a trip every few months and going to the doctor's or the hairdresser's in the day is just a dream. I like being able to pop and see my dad for lunch if I finish early or pick my niece up from school. They are the moments that really matter in life, hey? And I love that mid-afternoon fresh air . . . I love getting involved in initiatives and projects for women so I think that's where my work and life blends together. But when it comes to finishing work – I close my laptop, turn off my work phone and close the door to my office. Home time is home time. The best piece of advice I could give is to calculate your monthly living costs, times that by three and have that as your backup fund. I don't have a pension at the moment but I make sure I calculate how much tax I need to stash away each month and I have a separate business account that all my invoices get paid to. That way each month I just receive a salary like I would if I was employed.'

I loved hearing these stories, especially how different some of the mixes are and how they make it work. These accounts hammer home that there is no one-size-fits-all solution nor one answer, it's a personal and individual set-up, but there are lots and lots of people who are making it work and mixing and matching their careers. And you can do it too. Keep reading for more practical examples and tips in the coming chapters on blending work and home, avoiding burnout, money and the toolkit (Chapter 7).

CHAPTER 4

Our New Work Self

One of the most frequently asked questions I get is along the lines of: 'If I was going to lead a multi-hyphenate lifestyle, what impact would that have on my sense of self, or identity?' Because let's face it, a lot of us hide behind a fancy job title because it makes us feel good. But with many jobs dissolving and becoming irrelevant in a new world of work, these factors could easily impact our career identities. I get asked how to go about introducing or explaining what you do in social or networking situations. It's a good question, because you don't technically have just one main job, so what *do* you do? How can you feel the same amount of external self-worth if you don't have a big impressive one-liner to fall back on? When discussing the pros and cons of being a multi-hyphenate, it crops up time and time again as a concern. Perhaps you are worried that your work identity might feel weaker if you are not married to one company. A lot of who we are is tied up in our workplace roles whether we like it or not. It's clear that our work is connected to how we perceive ourselves and our purpose in the world (be it in a practical or even more spiritual sense). (You'll find more on the practicalities of networking in Chapter 9.)

What Do You Do?

When did our identities get so wrapped up in work? It makes sense that we place so much importance on it as we spend so much time at work and in the company of colleagues, of course it shapes us. But I argue that leading a multi-hyphenate lifestyle allows you to fully explore all areas of your personality. You can have a more rounded identity because you are reaching into hidden corners and introducing yourself as a *person*, not as a floating job title. It paves the way for more authentic connections, too.

This fear of how we explain our job proves just how much we care about how others perceive us and how much we now live in a sound-bite culture. We can sell ourselves in tweets, have a sharp LinkedIn bio, write a catchy email subject. Anything that takes too long to explain will probably have no listeners left. We want a strong elevator pitch and we don't have any time to waste. The thing is, having a few different hyphens to your CV means you can't necessarily sum up what you do very quickly or easily. It takes time, or you have to choose which hat to lead with. It's a strategy to know which bits of your bio are specifically relevant in certain situations. Being a multi-hyphenate means you are less fully attached to one sole career identity and therefore you should care less about how you come across when describing your job. Yes, you are less easily identified, summed up or placed in a neat box. Work up your own elevator pitch that succinctly sums up what you do, drawing in links between the hyphens (see below). It helps to have umbrella terms to sum things up. For me, I say that I'm an author and broadcaster. Under 'author' I can list writing books, magazine articles and blog posts and 'broadcaster' houses radio, podcasting and TV work. Loads of hyphens, but described under only two job career roofs.

TIPS FOR WRITING DOWN YOUR OWN ELEVATOR PITCH

1. Write down what you do, including all the hyphens.
   Example: At the moment I'm doing 'x', but I'm also working on 'y'
2. Sum them up all together as one spear-headed mission statement.
   Example: On the whole, my mission is to . . .
3. Speak more about *why* you love or do what you do (people like to hear the *why* in career scenarios).
   Example: I love these jobs/this mixture of careers because . . . and it allows me to do . . .

Since the launch of social media and designing our own online profiles, we now have an online personality whether we like it or not. When people scoff at the idea of having an online personal brand, they might not be aware that even by simply having a public Facebook or Instagram page you are essentially a brand. You have a bio, a profile picture, a mission and content. We have many different sides to us online: multiple contradicting interests, many different opinions, we tweet from the sofa at home, we answer online polls, we share our political beliefs in a Facebook status and project our hopes and dreams on our blogs or Pinterest feed. We are publishers of our own corners of the Internet. Yes, our digital footprint might be scrutinised occasionally, but mostly we are curating our online worlds as we go.

Living in this Twitter bio culture you must be immediately impressive. It matters how quickly we make an impression online, in our photos, bios and our words. We have more and more competition for people's time, attention and eyeballs on something. According to researchers at the Missouri University of Science and Technology 'it takes less than two-tenths of a second for an online visitor to form a first opinion of your brand once they've perused your company's website. And it takes just another 2.6 seconds for that viewer's eyes to concentrate in a way that reinforces that first impression.'[1]

I used to feel like I had to be or sound impressive the minute I walked into a room otherwise I wasn't succeeding. This was a huge eye-opener to me when I quit my job working at Condé Nast. I used to be able to walk into a room, introduce myself and people would be immediately impressed because they could place me with a big household media name and this made it easier to mingle. But now I prefer the challenge of truly connecting with people while also using my own elevator pitch to sell myself and my work.

Even though I am happier and richer (in all senses of the word), it is harder to sum up what I do and to give people an immediate context to my work. It means I don't have an easy, lazy way out. I don't cut corners when I introduce myself and expect people to know what I do. Instead, I have a string of work interests and hobbies and it doesn't matter if people don't find it impressive. The main thing is that I enjoy it and I make money from it – our hyphens are a personal relationship that we have with the world and what we do.

In an interview in the *Atlantic*, the author of *Do What You Love: And Other Lies about Success and Happiness*, Miya Tokumitsu, said: 'I've tried this little experiment when I meet people in non-work situations and try to see how long I can talk to them without asking about their work or have them ask me about my work. It's actually really hard to last longer than four minutes.' It is clear we are *all* tied to our jobs one way or another – we want to know when it comes to other people so we can have an idea of who someone is. It's a natural question. But having multiple hyphens allows you to have a bit of distance between your job and who you are. You are a mixture of things. We are all much more than just our job title.

I was thinking about how social media has perhaps made us braver and more open when it comes to being ourselves. Our phones know more intimate details about us than our partners do, some studies say. When it comes to the workplace, I think our thoughts, opinions, interests, personality traits matter more than ever. We are now more able to present our full selves. It's more difficult now to have a work self and an at-home self.

It's Not Just About Branding Yourself But Rebranding Yourself As You Go

There are dangers of becoming too attached to your Internet self. It means you end up spending too much time online because you like how your online self makes you feel and appear to the world. Your online self can feel more popular than you are in real life. However, in most jobs now (and in our leisure time) we do spend a disproportionate amount of time online, it's something that most of us end up doing. It's hard not to. However, a benefit of the Internet is that you can brand or rebrand anything online. You can make something a reality that IRL would be tricky (opening a shop, getting funding, creating a product, finding an audience in order to sell something niche). A company that has started to slowly descend in popularity and profit can get a new lease of life online with a shiny new website, marketing campaign, PR, storytelling or employees with an online following. According to *Business Today*, Starbucks 'pulled itself out of the financial meltdown of 2008 by aligning its operations with customer demands through social media.' They launched a multilingual Facebook page to deal with customer service issues across all platforms and offer recipes and tips on their popular YouTube channel. An internationally renowned company came close to financial collapse in 2003–2004 and was given a new lease of life by big social-media collaborations and film franchises; it is now thriving. The Help Refugees charity started off with just one hashtag #HelpCalais used by a few people. This hashtag has now grown into a million-pound official charity in just a couple of years.

The same can happen with a person who wants to form a new career. Think about exploring different platforms that might elevate you. The Internet allows you to sell yourself and your products in whatever way you want to. Tech has allowed anyone to put whatever they want into the world. It is possible to get noticed from any small seed online. The myth is that we have to have just one self or even just one Internet self but we can actually have many different projects on the go at once.

Will Storr, the author of *Selfie: How We Became So Self-Obsessed and What It's Doing to Us* speaks about 'the blank slate view' in his work. The definition of this view is that anyone can achieve anything. That everyone starts off with the same blank slate: 'It is instinctively, addictively attractive to people because we want to believe that anyone can achieve anything. It's a lovely story, and it's one our culture tells us repeatedly. But it's not true.'[2] Of course it's not true that everyone has the same start in life or the ability to start from the same place. The general thinking has been that some people are better placed than others to succeed. But that notion is changing. Decades ago, getting into a competitive industry really was impossible without knowing someone or having an 'in'. However, I do think that in this Internet age it is more likely that anyone can achieve anything. Our voices can rise up to the top more easily. We have the best possible chance, at least. The old gatekeepers are slowly disappearing. It is a lot more likely that you can achieve something now than before the Internet. Before social media, before this age where everyone can connect with anyone at the click of a button, it really did matter who you knew. The world is still full of huge inequalities, but I do believe that tech has allowed us to get our own foot in the door. I hope it continues to open more doors.

Having a Whole Sense of Self Matters

Having a multi-hyphenate job title allows me to feel as though I am being myself. I feel like I don't have that much of a separation between work and play because I am merging myself

across the two. I am multiple personalities and all those different selves have different needs. This is the same for you. A
multi-hyphenate career nurtures and nourishes these selves
and brings out our best skills and abilities.

You might totally cringe at the idea of someone knowing
the real you at work, because you'd rather get your stuff done
and leave. I used to be that person, too, and when my boss
(female) used to quiz me on my dating life during a meeting
I wanted to curl up and disappear into another dimension
like in *Stranger Things.* When it comes to the self in relation
to work, who we are and what we believe has a huge part to
play, in and out of the office. It's harder to keep 'work you'
and 'personal you' separate because of social media infiltrat-
ing all areas of our lives. I think we should be inspiring and
encouraging young people to be more themselves at work.
By being yourself, you are more likely to expose a super-
power that would benefit the workplace, for example, being
opinionated, active, being a good public speaker or having
any kind of hidden talent that would benefit your role at
work.

Social media has meant that we are more likely to merge
our work and personal selves online. We might tweet, Facebook
or Instagram about both work and home in the space of
minutes. The Internet has allowed us to express so many
different sides of ourselves: our hobbies, kids, pets, interests,
career choices. It can offer a holistic perspective of our life.
We in turn can 'online stalk' our colleagues and find out
contradictory things about them. It's like seeing your teacher
outside of school when you were a kid and they were in their
normal clothes and thinking, *Oh my God you're actually a*

person who does person things. It's hard to keep things separate now, even if we wanted to.

There's this phrase that has been doing the rounds: 'Bring your whole self to work.' Mike Robbins did a Tedx talk in Berkeley in 2015 with this exact title. But what does it mean? In his talk Mike said:

> For organisations, particularly in the twenty-first century, what it really takes for us to be fulfilled and successful is an ability to bring our whole selves to work. All of who we are. All the gifts, all the talents, the fears, the doubts, the insecurities, the things that matter most. But what that involves for us as individuals and organisations of various sizes, is actually a lot of courage.'

Essentially it means not hiding away from awkward conversations. It means having human-to-human conversations about when life gets in the way and having real conversations with colleagues about things. I've found in my multi-hyphenate career I've finally been able to bring my whole self to my job. The multiple sides of my personality come out and offer different skills in different situations, with different people.

Being Our Real Selves at Work is Very Important

Kenji Yoshino at NYU School of Law and Christie Smith, Managing Principal, Deloitte University Leadership Center for Inclusion released a paper called 'A new model of inclusion' all about how allowing and encouraging people to be their real selves at work will help achieve more diversity within companies.

The findings suggest that hiding your real self could hold you back in the workplace, when really you're expecting the opposite effect. We assume hiding our real selves will help us get ahead. We are often afraid of being unique, standing out or upsetting the status quo. We think that hiding away our real selves might help us blend in and get ahead but in fact we need to be *more* ourselves.

The study revealed some very unfortunate reasons why some people feel the need to hide parts of themselves at work: 'Women might say they are rushing off to an offsite meeting instead of saying they are picking up their sick child from school, for fear of being taken less seriously than childless colleagues.'[3] Reading that some women pretend not to be a mother at work is an awful realisation. It shows that the stigma is still very much real. Leading the multi-hyphenate life encourages complexity and multitudes, you are allowed to embrace all sides of yourself, you don't have to hide anything because you are functioning in a way that suits you. You can be your full self with no exceptions.

Not being our true selves at work also means we are not able to bond with our colleagues as much because we are only giving half of ourselves away. It means we need to work harder to get a boss or colleague to buy in because they only know half the story.

Hiding parts of ourselves and our identity is not just about personality either. '29% of respondents said they hide aspects of their appearance. Women reported wearing clothes that are more masculine because they feel their colleagues will be more likely to take them seriously.'[4] We should be able to bring in other aspects of ourselves into the workplace and for it to improve our working life and enable us to make strong bonds with colleagues and clients. It's about exploring different aspects of ourselves that showcase what we could bring to work and hopefully means we are seen in a more open-minded way.

There are benefits to be being yourself at work in terms of overall well-being and productivity levels. Hiding ourselves or pretending to be someone else is not going to be beneficial to the company or to ourselves in the long run.

Personal Branding Isn't New

You probably find the phrase 'personal branding' a bit irritating by now. But a lot of what we do is so dependent on our brand. Personal branding is being treated like something new, but it's not new at all. It's always been there, for decades, centuries even. Your name is your brand and what you do that is specifically *you* is the reason people pick you for the job. Who you are has always mattered, but in the age of social media it matters so much more. Your Google page is your CV. Your Twitter bio is your elevator pitch. Your website is your shop window. Your choice of font matters. Everything online is selling who you are. You have a brand even if you've never been on the Internet in your life, but if you are going to play the Internet game you definitely need to work on a strong brand identity for you and your work.

According to Cecile Alper-Leroux, vice president of HCM innovation at Ultimate Software, 'We were observing, through conversations with our customers, as well as media coverage, that something was happening in the world regarding the way people identify themselves in relation to their employment. Where someone works is much less relevant to employees' identities.'[5] So we place less importance on our job to tell the story of who we are and I think that is a positive thing. It means we will not take a job just because of what it will look like on paper nor because of social pressures. We will pick jobs because we feel that they suit us. We have more freedom now, to explore lots of different avenues, to try out different sides of our personality.

THREE TIPS ON BRANDING YOUR PERSONAL ONLINE SPACE

1. **Be visible:** It's important when building a brand to be visible consistently over time. Make sure you are regularly posting at a time where people can see you. This will differ from person to person, but you can use a tool like Iconosquare to help you find your best times to post. Quality over quantity is important, but repetition of what works is key.

2. **Have a strong USP:** Like any brand, pinpoint what makes you different. Stand out from your peers. Dig into the real reason you are doing what you're doing. Think about the title of the Paul Arden book – *Whatever You Think, Think the Opposite*. Thinking the opposite is a good exercise to challenge yourself and your first instincts. We naturally go along with what the trends are and what other people are doing, but

challenge yourself to brainstorm ideas that go against the norms.

3. **Collaborate:** Work with and alongside people you admire, who share the same ethics and values as you. The people you choose to work with reflects on you and your brand.

THE REAL REASON PERSONAL BRANDING IS HERE TO STAY

Building a personal brand is not a vanity project. It's not about Instagram followers or even about looking good. It's about the new trend towards talent retention. Because of the Internet, your job is now not as safe as it once was and you are in competition with anyone who has the skill set to do your job, not just your colleagues. Before the Internet and in the early online days you didn't have to worry about this so much. Your job for life could be a job for life because there was minimal chance anyone would steal it or that the company's recruitment would happen out of a global pool of people. Things have changed. *New York Times* columnist Tom Friedman makes a good point: 'If you have a challenge that's posed to you, why in the world would you limit yourself simply to the talent within your own company? Because the odds of it being the best in this world are really pretty low.'[6] Companies now want to recruit contractors and experts and hire them on specific projects. Employing someone full-time might not make sense in the future as companies change and grow so quickly. They are more likely to recruit externally and see who the best people are on a case-by-case basis. This of course sounds scary, unless you have prepared for it.

Personal branding is the best strategy for your multi-hyphenate career because the percentage of people in your network who know who you are and what you do will increase, which means more business. In the future when the majority of people are contractors and solo workers and companies outsource more than hire full-time, you will want to stand out, whether your skills are niche or very broad or a combination. It's not who you know, but who knows you.

FIVE REASONS PERSONAL BRANDING ISN'T GOING AWAY

1. **We live in an increasingly visual world:** It's important that people can easily distinguish the look and feel of your work in a sea of other competitors.
2. **Online profiles are here to stay:** We might change social platforms in the future, there might be many new ones that replace our much-loved platforms right now, but our personal brand will evolve and live on over time. Our brand will remain, even when platforms or apps change.
3. **We need to build more trust:** Working on your brand that feels 100% real is an important step in the future of the Internet and online workplace. Personal brands are important because we make decisions on people.
4. **The future of recruitment:** Many companies already recruit solely using online search on candidates, so being in control of your online brand is really crucial to how you attract new work.
5. **How to attract genuine connections:** With a strong, real online brand, people can understand you, your intentions, motivations and your work in a matter of seconds. It means we can connect with like-minded people or search out the right people for a project or the best new hire for a team more easily.

> 'The employer or industry will no longer be the centre of your career – you will be' – Gwendolyn Parkin, director of IntegralCareer

The Art of Self-Promoting Without Selling Your Soul

With the rise of the online entrepreneur, self-promotion has become a new normal to us. Doing an Instagram story directing people to our new project is commonplace. But is this work or is this play? As a society, we are now rewarded for being seen. Likes, comments, followers, they turn into something tangible. Followers turn into money, whether it's free clothes, free luxury trips abroad or eyeballs on our work. Our following has value. Are you more likely to get a part in a film or a book deal if you have more followers? Probably. Is that fair? No. But we are social animals who enjoy being seen, feeling like we matter and we can't help but explore the different ways we can get higher in the status chain. Therefore, we aren't necessarily to blame if we have fallen into the trap of needing to self-promote ourselves to get ahead, especially if we have tangible results at the end of it. Now, there's a difference between bragging and promoting. It's the climate we live in and we can see that it needs to be done. You simply cannot get more work without promoting yourself. You are a business and you need to market yourself in any way you can. But we don't need to constantly brag or plug away, this will have the adverse effect and you will have no one left to promote to!

TIPS FOR SELF-PROMOTING WITHOUT FEELING ICKY

- **Ask yourself why:** Make sure people know *why* you are promoting the thing you are promoting. Is it because you're proud, happy, worried, wanting something specific, or even openly needing the money? It makes the promoting come across as more human and open instead of just broadcasting something for no reason or hiding the root causes from your friends or followers.

- **Make something you like or would be interested in yourself:** Be proud of what you are sharing. This seems obvious, but if you make/build/launch something that *you* like, promoting it will feel natural and you'll be excited to share it, not embarrassed.

- **Use *your* voice:** The most distinctive way of promoting your work is by speaking in your voice. Write in a way that feels as close to your speaking voice as you can. Forcing yourself to be overly 'authentic' can end up being a false version of authenticity. It's best to imagine you are speaking to people IRL and telling them in a conversational way about what you're doing.

- **Don't be too harsh on yourself:** You'd probably tell a friend to go for it or not overthink it or be less judgemental, so take your own advice. It's not the end of the world if something doesn't resonate, you can try something different tomorrow. Treat most things like it isn't a huge deal and you will take more small daily risks with the way you promote yourself. You might have a few mini failures and that's okay.

- **Talk to the right people:** Self-promotion hardly ever feels icky if you are talking to an audience that wants to hear from you. Email newsletters are a great way to build this small, connected audience. It's a group of people who are opted in. This way it feels less like you are broadcasting to an empty or busy room.

Why You Should Add a Self-Care Hyphen to Your Job Title

What if adding an extra hyphen to your life isn't actually about work at all? I received a book in the mail this year called *The Self-Care Project* by Jayne Hardy. On one of the first pages she said something I'd felt for so long myself about mental-health dips:

> I missed writing – it was something I'd always loved until depression sapped the joy and self-belief out of it for me. I decided that writing a beauty blog might help me with self-care. To write about beauty products I'd have to use beauty products – self-care right there! That little blog helped me in ways I'm not sure I can properly put into words; it gave me purpose, distracted me from the suicidal thoughts, injected pleasure back into writing, brought sunshine back into my life.

Adding personal hyphens into life can definitely be an act of self-care. Having a side-hustle is mainly described in a way that makes it sound like an aggressive business venture, but it doesn't always have to be. I have felt that having side-projects makes me feel creative on the side of many jobs that didn't. They allowed me to escape into something that is just mine and that I had total control over. Self-care can come in many forms and all that matters is that you are doing something that is purely for yourself and your own mental health or relaxation. It looks different to all of us, but allowing yourself time for something that sits outside of work and home to-do lists feels quite empowering and nourishing for the mind.

Doing something that we enjoy regularly isn't selfish or self-indulgent it's actually crucial to our overall well-being. In Tom Bath and Jim Carter's PhD paper 'Your Career, Well-Being and Your Identity' they sum up what basic well-being is: 'At a fundamental level, we all need something to do, and ideally something to look forward to, when we wake up every day.' When it comes to our careers, having something enjoyable on the side can really make a positive difference: 'If you don't have the opportunity to regularly do something you enjoy – even if it's more of a passion or interest than something you get paid to do – the odds of you having high well-being in other areas diminish rapidly.'

The *New York Times* recently did a feature on burnout, that phrase we all know too well (and there is a whole chapter on it to follow), especially in this modern-day working world where we can easily work 24/7 if we're not careful. In the *NYT* article it stated that one of the ways to combat burnout at work is 'a hobby outside of work through which you can decompress, de-stress and dissociate from work.'[7] Finding something to turn to that relaxes you is important and doesn't need to have a bigger agenda beyond that.

Self-care is much more than buying a few material things every now and again. The *hygge* trend received some backlash as the Danish ritual of enjoying life's simple pleasures turned into a huge money-maker. Buying an expensive candle or faux-fur rug became an emblem of self-care. Of course truly taking care of yourself goes deeper than a Body Shop splurge. We have to make sure that self-care runs into the crevices of our lifestyles, making us able to function better and giving us time to realise we matter, our brain and body matter, and that we should find time to like ourselves among the business.

In one study, research scientist Zorana Ivcevic Pringle found that people who engaged in everyday forms of creativity such as taking photographs, making a collage or publishing in a literary magazine tended to be more open-minded, curious, positive, energetic and motivated by their activity. The forms of everyday creativity also led to increased feelings of well-being and personal satisfaction compared to fellow classmates who were less engaged in everyday creative activities.[8]

The old assumption that 'creativity' equals having some element of 'madness' turns out not to be necessarily true either. Earlier this year a study found that GPs prescribing arts activities to their patients resulted in a significant drop in hospital admissions and therefore saved the NHS money.[9] Having a hyphen that allows you to be more creative, open up more, exercise those muscles you don't use in other aspects of your life could be life-changing. Having something that you do that makes you feel more like the best version of yourself can add to feelings of confidence and with this increase in confidence it's more likely that doors will open for you. With your own multi-hyphenated mix you are less likely to get FOMO, because you know you are in your own lane and on your own journey.

CHAPTER 5

Burnout Culture

First of all, can I admit something to you? I love Urban Dictionary. I often prefer its definitions and colloquial language over standard dictionaries. It feels more real (and funny and obviously occasionally very rude). When I typed in 'burnout' it came up with this:

> A state of emotional and physical exhaustion caused by a prolonged period of stress and frustration; an inevitable corporate condition characterised by frequent displays of unprofessional behaviour, a blithe refusal to do any work, and most important, a distinct aura of not giving a shit.

This is true – this is how I define and detect burnout when it comes to my own behaviour. If I have lost interest, am cancelling exciting meetings because of anxiety, become snappy with my colleagues and friends or have a glazed-over aura of not caring about my career, I know burnout is upon me. I know that I need to seriously change my ways, back off and prioritise and protect my mental health. And take some sort of action.

Of course I should include the official definition of burn-out too, according to psychologist David Ballard, PsyD, MBA: 'Burn-out can be defined as "an extended period of time where someone experiences exhaustion and a lack of interest in things".'[1]

I haven't always been a multi-hyphenate waving the flag for flexibility. I worked in a rigid, non-flexible structure for years because I didn't know there was any other option. There's a lack of knowledge about what different jobs are out there and that flexibility is available. (And another part of the problem is still a lingering stigma when it comes to anyone who works in a different way from the norm.) According to a report from Timewise in 2017, there are '8.7 million people who don't currently work flexibly, but would like to if the jobs were there'. In my fast-paced job working for a top media company, I started to realise how ill I was getting due to the long hours and the stress of relentlessly demanding bosses. I had an old boss who shouted 'YOU CAN SLEEP WHEN YOU'RE DEAD' at me whenever I complained about being a bit overworked. I was so stressed in one job that I started getting nocturnal anxiety (yes, when you go to the toilet about eighteen times a night, not normal for a twenty-something). I went to the doctor and my bladder was fine – it was the anxiety. I would also get cystitis because I was so busy I would forget to go to the toilet. These are two extreme examples, but some of our stresses can go unnoticed for months, or even years. It's no surprise that burnout is on the rise. We are in the midst of combating our fears of becoming irrelevant in a world that is changing so rapidly. In general, people and society fear change. We fear changing our lives and the model that has existed for ever. People fear that changing their careers means starting all over again. But the pace of work is changing and moving to a new job doesn't necessarily mean going backwards or having to study and retrain. A lot of the new digital jobs simply require getting your hands dirty.

Right now, we are more anxious than ever. According to PwC, 'More than a third of the UK workforce is experiencing anxiety, depression, or stress, according to a survey of employees in junior and senior roles.' The study also says that of those employees who have taken time off due to the stress and anxiety '39 per cent said they did not feel comfortable telling their employer about the issue.'[2] We might be talking about it to our friends in the pub or in anonymous forums, but we don't seem to be openly discussing it in the workplace. We are oversharing in other ways though: tweeting what we had for breakfast, blogging about our sex lives and sharing our temporary profile pictures on Facebook that show which political party we vote for. But it seems that our relationship with our work and the anxieties it can present is still quite a closed subject and is hard to talk about in detail.

While Instagram presents a rosy take on life, in conversations with my friends in private WhatsApp groups we are open about our anxieties and fears. Our truth comes out in what Alexis C. Madrigal coined as 'dark social', which is the private messaging we do. The term 'dark traffic' is also an interesting one, described as 'the result of people sharing website links through email, text messages and private chats'. So the conversation is happening, and the links are being shared, but in private messaging, so we can't always see it. What we see on public profiles is a very small piece of the pie.

Fears of redundancy, fears of not working hard enough, fears of working too hard and heading towards burnout, fears of moving into the freelance life and fears of not having the courage to move jobs or start a side-hustle – it seems we are in need of guidance and no-holds-barred honesty on how to head towards a healthy work-life balance. Some of us live to work, some work to live. But there is one thing we have in common and that's how plugged in we all are now. I'm particularly interested in how we can try and make technology work for us, not against us, in allowing us to have more freedom and to be less burned out and stressed.

The Multi-Hyphen Method is not about working long hours. It's about short, productive bursts. More breaks, more bursts of energy. It's a different way of working. This of course goes against the many assumptions about multi-hyphenates, that we are workaholics who burn ourselves out by working all week and then working a side gig at the weekend.

The General Social Survey of 2016, a nationwide survey that since 1972 has tracked the attitudes and behaviours of American society, found that 50 per cent of respondents were consistently exhausted because of work, compared with 18 per cent two decades earlier.[3] Is tech to blame? Possibly. There's no denying the importance of tech, but are we in dire need of work boundaries set by our employers? Do we need our employers to lead by example? I think so.

According to a new infographic in the US created by Eastern Kentucky University, companies spend $300 billion annually for healthcare and missed work days as a result of workplace stress.[4] That's what happens when you push and push and keep asking for more from people inside a rigid structure. Asking for flexible working hours can change the way we work and the limits we set on ourselves. The work will get done, but in less restrictive circumstances. We must trust our employees to get work done, in their own way. Since working in this new multi-hyphenate way, it has allowed me to put ring fences around each project and manage having more days off. Since reading that our brains can focus on any given task for 90–120 minutes, first discovered by Nathan Kleitman, a groundbreaking researcher, I ring-fence my time in spurts. I don't think, *What can I get done in this* entire *day?* Instead I think, *What can I achieve in ninety-minute sessions with breaks in between?* I work fewer hours than my pre-multi-hyphenate days and get more done because I do it at times of my own peak productivity. Some days I will get more done in one ninety-minute burst than I do if I work a whole day non-stop.

Technology has blurred the lines between work and play more than ever and it's opened up brand-new conversations, both good (flexibility!) and bad (burn-out). A 2018 long read in the *Guardian* said: 'Technology was supposed to liberate us from much of the daily slog, but has often made things worse: in 2002, fewer than 10% of employees checked their work email outside of office hours. Today, with the help of tablets and smartphones, it is 50%, often before we get out of bed.'[5] We need to start having these sorts of conversations with friends and colleagues and it's important, now more than ever, to admit we are overwhelmed. It's also important that we're not afraid to say, 'I don't know where I'm going in my career' or 'I feel like I'm wasting time online'. It's okay to feel confused right now, but it's time to take matters into your own hands if you are feeling jaded or let down. It's not about turning your back on traditional employment, but it is about doing your own thing on the side and wrapping a layer of empowerment and protection around yourself in this unstable jobs market. At a time of vulnerability, we need to use the tools we have and do the best we can. But we also need to learn what our own personal boundaries and limits are while doing so. What tips us over the edge? How much can we do without starting to go downhill? What does balance actually look like to each of us? Has the limit of what we can cope with changed?

Burnout is real. Technology still sometimes feels like an exciting midnight feast that we want to binge on. It's here and it's hovering all around us. Most of us are probably on the edge of burnout, have experienced it at some point or watched a friend suffer because of it. It is when you push and push, with very little left in the tank and then you hit zero. You hit minus figures. You use every scrap of reserved petrol in the tank. Burnout takes over and mentally or physically affects us for a while until we have more petrol in the tank again.

HOW TO SPOT BURNOUT

- Noticing yourself being really cynical about everyone and everything
- Becoming more apathetic than usual, not caring that much about the outcome of a project

- When tasks that were quite easy become difficult or overwhelming
- Physical symptoms – illnesses, weak immune system, aches or pains
- Isolating yourself and feeling a huge loss of energy

HOW TO AVOID BURNOUT IF YOU SPOT TELLTALE SIGNS

- Prioritise your sleep (and I recommend curling up with the book *Why We Sleep* by Matthew Walker)
- Start saying 'no' more often, however difficult that might be
- Cancel any plans that are making you feel anxious
- Focus on important aspects of a to-do list and don't over-work yourself on extra things for the sake of it
- Practise self-care, whether that's getting more fresh air and alone time, or doing a creative hobby that relaxes you
- Take a step back, write down the things that are stressing you out. Bullet journals can help with this exercise
- Lie in bed for a few minutes each morning without immediately checking your phone
- Break up anything that is overwhelming you into small, bite-size chunks

It's Time to Get Rid of Sleep Stigma

We can't help it but we often judge people who prioritise sleep. Someone recently said to me: 'We don't call babies lazy when they sleep all the time, they are growing!' Sleep is so important. According to the US National Heart, Lung, and Blood Institute (NHLBI), 'Sleep deficiency can lead to physical and mental health problems, injuries, loss of productivity, and even a greater risk of death.' So why do we still think we don't need much of it and that work can encroach on this precious commodity?

I am personally a big fan of naps. Sometimes when I admit this, I feel like I might be judged for it because we appear culturally allergic to sleeping. Naps are normally thought of as for the lazy and unambitious. But I've found there have been so many benefits to napping when it comes to life and work. I can work longer and I feel more refreshed after one. I feel more in control of my life and schedule. I break up the day. Scientists have shown that a sixty to ninety-minute siesta can charge up the brain's batteries as much as eight hours tucked up in bed.[6]

Nap classes have popped up at spas and gyms and in Madrid, Spain, a nap bar has opened called Siesta & Go (what a great name). Of course in Spain it is culturally the norm to nap in the afternoon but imagine if this was available for everyone everywhere! On arrival you can choose from a menu of options in either private or shared rooms. Naps can be booked by the minute or hour, costing between €8 (one hour in a bunk) to €14 for an hour in a segregated room. You can book or walk in off the street. Genius.

More than 85% of mammalian species are what's called 'polyphasic sleepers' which means they sleep for short bursts throughout the day instead of in one block like humans do, suggesting that our sleep routine isn't in keeping with other mammals.[7] Eleanor Roosevelt, Winston Churchill, Leonardo da Vinci and Albert Einstein are all famous nappers.[8]

In his book *Why We Sleep*, Matthew Walker actually uncovers that lack of sleep is deadly and he calls people who boast about not sleeping the 'sleepless elite'. He told the Business Insider that 'Sleep deprivation depletes stores of your "natural killer cells," a type of lymphocyte (white blood cell) that nix tumour and virus cells. A single 4- or 5-hour night of sleep could lower your body's "natural killer" cell count by around 70%.'[9] Lack of sleep is literally killing us.

Another consideration is how tech affects our sleep patterns. According to sleep.org, about 72 per cent of children age six to seventeen sleep with at least one electronic device in their bedroom. The blue light from our phones suppresses melatonin production, the bright lights keep our brains alert and not to mention the lights, vibrations and sounds that can keep waking us up throughout the night.

Hobbies are Not the Same as Side-Hustles

Burnout can rear its ugly head by overstretching yourself. One thing to flag is that not everything should turn into a money-making, scheming side-hustle. Some things should be kept sacred and purely for leisure. Having something you enjoy does not instantly mean you should try and turn it into a business venture. For example, if you are someone that loves taking baths, it doesn't mean you necessarily need to launch a side-hustle selling bath products online. I mean, you *could*, but you might also just love taking baths as part of your much-needed leisure time. Pinpoint the difference. Protect your hobbies. (But if you have a skill or interest outside of work that you feel you could also monetise in some way, then that's great too!)

How Job-Sharing Can Free You Up and Broaden Your Horizons

Let's talk for a moment about job-sharing. This set-up can allow you to work flexibly in a job role and allow you to take on your other hyphens outside of the office. In a former workplace of mine, two editors at a magazine shared a job. One worked Monday and Tuesday, the other Wednesday, Thursday, Friday. They swapped over the work on email and in phone calls. They got their routine down. They made it as seamless as possible and had each other's backs. I observed their system and was in awe at the way they made it work. The work always got done and it was done really well. In a job-share your boss is winning too, they technically get two brains for the price of one. Yes, these editors got half the wages, but in their days off they did other freelance work or hobbies or duties that fulfilled them in different ways and were other possible streams of income. It meant they were both keeping their options open, meeting new contacts and making extra money, all while holding down a day job that didn't make them tear their hair out and paid the bills.

I interviewed Lindsay Frankel, a journalist at *The Times* and an ex-colleague of mine. Lindsay also job-shared in the same office as me and it looked like it was working for her. I found it really inspiring when I discovered that Lindsay actively put herself forward for the opportunity to job-share. She said, 'I didn't ever think it was an option for me as I don't have children.' I asked how she was able to ask for this set-up as it's still not seen as the 'norm'. She commented:

> It was the editor offering it up that made me consider I could be eligible. And once I got the job it opened my eyes to the fact that I could be more available to my elderly mum or just spend better time with my niece and nephew (like picking them up from school on a Monday because I didn't have to race back to London after a weekend visiting). Just not work all the time like I had done for the past twenty years. It's not just parents who benefit from flexibility.

As someone currently without children, I often felt judged for wanting flexibility and a multi-hyphenate career with days 'off'. I asked her if she had any advice on making a job-share work for anyone who might be considering it: 'Don't be competitive. I think this is vital. I didn't want the whole job, neither did she. I didn't try to be her and vice versa. I think this meant we could trust each other. I can't imagine job-sharing with someone you thought was trying to shaft you!'

HOW TO MAKE JOB-SHARING WORK

After interviewing Lindsay and speaking to friends who successfully job-share, here is a pie-chart presenting my take on what's required, to be taken as a loose starting point.

What's required for successful job-sharing

Don't be competitive (16%)

Collaboration (20%)

Constant communication (16%)

Honesty (16%)

Don't dump stuff on each other (16%)

Work ethic (16%)

Glorifying 'Busy' is Bad for Us

Long hours without breaks means we run out of energy and concentration. How can any human being be expected to work solidly for an extremely long period of time? We know we can't and yet we push through and do just that. Talking to friends of mine who are lawyers and doctors, it is clear that overworking leads to resentment and mistakes and productivity drops. The Japanese have an actual word for 'death by overworking' – *karōshi*. The major medical causes of *karōshi* deaths are heart attacks and strokes due to stress and starvation. This phenomenon is also widespread in South Korea, where it is referred to as *gwarosa*. In China, overwork-induced death is called *guolaosi*.

Consultant Cali Williams Yost says:

> But working harder and faster in the hopes of staying safe can be counterproductive. You neglect your health. You don't sleep or eat well. You don't exercise or take a vacation to recharge. You don't nurture your professional network or your personal support system. But your boss can't tell you when to focus on the parts of life that keep you healthy and happy.[10]

Just because we *can* do more, doesn't mean we should.

The metric of success used to be 'busy'. It still is, in some ways. The ideal worker has to look like they are doing the most in order to be congratulated. I recognise this because I worked in this sort of environment for years. We feel as though every single moment of time needs to be filled to the brim in order to get the most out of every second of every day. However, being busy all the time is certainly not allowing us to be creative.

Being busy is still something that people like to brag about. Yahoo's Marissa Mayer told Bloomberg News that she used to work 130-hour work weeks.[11] Most 'successful' people profiled in *Stylist* magazine get up at 6 a.m. and often work into the evening. Apple CEO Tim Cook told *Time* magazine once that he begins his day at 3.45 a.m.[12] It seems odd that working insane hours is still something to brag about, that it's still seen in some way as equalling success. However, slowly this is changing.

Human beings aren't meant to always be on. I love this quote: 'There is literally nothing in nature that blooms all year long so do not expect yourself to do so.' It reminds us that we are organisms that need to rest and grow.

I love Laura Archer's book *Gone for Lunch: 52 Things to do in Your Lunch Break* and the accompanying campaign to actually get people to eat their lunch. This break is an important time to fuel your mind and body for phase two of the working day.

HERE'S SOME STEPS I TAKE TO EARN MORE AND WORK LESS

- **Cut down on travel time:** Do not waste time travelling to meetings throughout the day. Either plan all your meetings in one part of the day or have conversations on Skype or Google Hangout. Fiercely protect your commute time.
- **Clear parameters on time and fee:** Always be very clear on how long something will take you to complete. If you're unsure, never pick a ballpark figure out of the air for the whole project, break down your fee by hour or day or half day. It means you won't do extra work for free. Value your time.
- **Outsource your administrative tasks:** A PA used to be something that only a high-powered CEO would have, but not any more. Virtual assistants can help with tasks that can suck your time, for example: data entry, transcription, scheduling, copywriting, programming, design. Virtual PAs

are great because they can do the work as and when (they don't necessarily need to be retained) and they usually work at home and in fact they may never meet their clients in person.

Know Your Own Limits

Our susceptibility to burnout and our energy limits might be different to our friends or colleagues. This is why work-shaming anyone isn't a good thing. Work-shaming is when you make someone feel bad for their work choices, even branding someone a 'workaholic' isn't exactly supportive. There's no one solution for everyone. It's really down to the individual's limits. Telling a friend to work less or slow down might be counter-intuitive as they may be having a positive energetic flow of work and it doesn't necessarily mean they are burning out. Whereas you could hit burnout by doing one thing too many (saying yes to too many nights out, for example). We all have a different idea of what balance is and it should be a personal journey in discovering it.

There is a tendency to make sweeping generalisations as to how we should deal with the overwhelming nature of social media and tech. There have been calls to ban under-eighteens from using social media without prior mental-health training courses on how to deal with the Internet because many people feel that young people are ill-equipped for online life.[13] It definitely makes sense to give mental-health training and have it available, but do we need to ban an entire age group from using social media? Surely it would make more sense to give young people more access to advice, tips and tools on how to deal with burnout or feeling overwhelmed instead of taking something away entirely. We know these are testing times and more mental-health training needs to be available: 'An estimated one in three teenage girls is reported as suffering from depression or anxiety, which is a rise of 10% on figures just 10 years ago.'

We need to get better at teaching ourselves and those around us to filter information effectively so that we are not overwhelmed by endless information. Tom Friedman said it well: 'the Internet, the mother of all flows, is actually an open sewer of untreated, unfiltered information.'[14] We are wading through so much rubbish online daily, no wonder it is making us exhausted. But there are some simple ways in which we can better manage our time spent online and combat the feeling of being overwhelmed.

HERE ARE SOME TIPS ON CURATING
YOUR ONLINE ENVIRONMENT

- 'Unfollow' or 'Mute' that annoying person or brand online that feels too intrusive. You aren't unfriending, it's not a cull, you are simply hiding it from your feed. You can also mute keywords on platforms like Twitter.
- Remove push notifications on apps you don't want daily (or hourly) updates from.
- Save articles you want to read into an app like Pocket (which you can also get as an extension on your browser) or instapaper.com so you can read everything at the end of the day or the next morning. This means you're not constantly consuming or getting notifications.

- Use simplenote.com to store notes across all your devices. It means you don't need to go on to your emails or online to send yourself a message which might end up distracting you with something else.
- Something like nuzzel.com helps you curate your own news discovery. You save time by getting the best and most relevant information sent straight to you.

Is Social Media the New Smoking?

'It's not hard for me to imagine that in 20 years from now we find that what social media does to our brains is equivalent to what smoking does to our lungs' – Yancey Strickler, – Kickstarter CEO[15]

I find myself sitting in a towel after I've got out of the shower, sat on my bed, scrolling in a loop, almost in a daze, unable to stop. This is the part that I'm not comfortable with. I love technology, my career is built around it, but it's about balance and not being a slave to tech and taking control of it. In order not to burn out it's important that we establish some ground rules when it comes to our tech. That doesn't mean undergoing extravagant digital-detox packages that are sold to us. We shouldn't have to spend £1,000 on a weekend away without our phone. It is too excessive and not accessible to most. Back when I worked at a well-known women's magazine, we would get pitched '10 ways to do a digital detox!' about twenty times a week. What irritated me about these ideas on how to switch off was they were always sugar-coated in something expensive: a yoga retreat, an expensive leather bag that turns off your notifications, a faraway health resort run by a wellness guru. It always seemed like a way to just rip people off and I wasn't convinced that any of these things were actually going to help us in our day-to-day lives. Switching off is more about how we handle a stressful Tuesday afternoon at work and not how to have an extravagant weekend away only to get cramps in your shoulders the minute you return. Call me old-fashioned, but I don't think mindfulness should have to come with a massive price tag.

It's the mindless scrolling that is the hard thing to kick to the curb. Leading a multi-hyphenate lifestyle involves a lot of self-motivation, so addressing your social-media scrolling addiction is crucial. To work less and earn more, it means being really strict with your social-media usage. It means scheduling content more than posting it manually.

It certainly feels like we are living in a time where everything is 'urgent'. Lynn Enright summed this up in a piece for The Pool: 'There is a lot of urgency around: there is a greedy internet to fill with content; there are other media outlets to best and beat; there are ideas, tidbits, pictures and rumours, on Twitter and in inboxes and WhatsApp groups, and they might be urgent, you've got to check.'[16] It feels so good to rebel against someone else's urgency, someone else's ASAP alerts. In order to make something that lives on, that might mean something or even make us money in the long run, we can't fall into the trap of wasting all of our time on Snapchat or Instagram Stories. Sometimes it can feel like we are hamsters trapped in a wheel, clicking on the content that we have to watch immediately otherwise it might disappear.

True productivity occurs when we are aware of what our bodies are doing. We waste time when we go and get that millionth coffee from the kitchen at work, we also waste time when we mindlessly scroll through social media.

Having a healthy relationship with our devices is about monitoring our time-wasting as it happens. Do you scroll and then realise a large chunk of time has just vanished? Do you go for an early night and find yourself reading the entire World Wide Web before bed? Do your eyes ache from too much screen time? Do your eyes glaze over? Do you find yourself looking at stuff that makes you feel bad about yourself? I think the way to address these behaviours is more about taking control of our daily lives than going cold turkey or 'curing' ourselves of our addictions. It's about realising when we are online too much, it's catching ourself while we're in the trap. It's being more mindful, it's stopping ourselves as we reach for our phones yet again and asking ourselves why we're doing it.

> The term 'addiction' is no exaggeration. We get hits of dopamine every time we get a like, comment or notification – many studies have said that we feel the same when we get a positive online notification as we do a hug. The average person checks his or her smartphone 150 times a day, making more than 2,000 swipes and touches.'[17]

The heaviest smartphone users click, tap or swipe on their phone 5,427 times a day, according to researcher Dscout.[18] Surely, being so addicted is not making us very productive in office spaces where we have to sit and work all day with constant distractions. We need to get better at disconnecting. However, if our attention spans are being diminished and we like to work on multiple things or having multiple metaphorical tabs open, then the rise of the Multi-Hyphen Method makes sense. It allows you to concentrate on one thing at a time, but you do jump on to the next thing quite quickly too, but all the while maintaining control. When working for yourself you're more aware of time and output, often because you are working on things yourself without a huge team. You're much less likely to want to spend precious hours wasting time on your phone because you're working on your own passion project, but I didn't mind scrolling through dead hours when there was nothing to do in the office.

There are, of course, interesting studies coming out about young people and tech. Shocking admissions are coming from ex-employees at tech giants who are confessing that they know how addictive their online products can be. One story emerged when the *Guardian* profiled Justin Rosenstein, an American software programmer who created the like button when he was an engineer at Facebook. The interview revealed a lot about the classic traps, like getting you to check your phone more often by spacing out push notifications and gamifying the experience of social networking (hearts, likes, polls, shares). It revealed that 'younger technologists are weaning themselves off their own products, sending their children to elite Silicon Valley schools where iPhones, iPads and even laptops are banned.'[19] Another former Facebook employee, Chamath Palihapitiya, who left in 2011, admitted that 'we have created tools that are ripping apart the social fabric of how society works.'[20] The creepiest bit was when he said that the mindless scrolling isn't something we've accidentally fallen into, it is apparently all 'just as their designers [at the tech giants] intended'. One positive that comes out of this honesty might be that younger generations will be more aware of the science behind the tech and the consequences of the way they use it. Self-awareness and self-analysis are the first steps to not letting tech control you as much. And being more aware of how the tech is actually made is the next step to avoiding being sucked into it for life. If you *know more* about the design or the way it's been built, we can take action to combat its influence. As Martha Lane Fox says: 'So let us educate our children by teaching them as much as we can about technology. We need to go beyond basic skills to raise the first generation of native digital understanders – people who, unlike most of the rest of us, know where and how their technology is made.'[21] In order to be truly empowered and emboldened by technology we have to understand it more deeply. Otherwise we are mindlessly becoming addicted and not looking beneath the surface as to what it's doing to us and why.

Endless scrolling through the news is also making a lot of us sick. The pace of information is relentless. Journalist Jess Commons recently wrote for Refinery29:

A few months ago, I, a fully grown-up, functional human woman, had to take nearly a month off work in the wake of the rising tensions between Kim Jong-un and Donald Trump. I know it sounds ridiculous to say out loud, but from the 'fire and fury' day, I was a mess. I spent days sitting on my couch, crying, not eating and watching

rubbish movies. No matter what anyone said to me, I
could not get my anxiety under control.[22]

Our phones can make brilliant things happen, but they can
also be the source of a lot of anxiety. It's time to take control.
We need to set our own personal limits and not feel bad for
switching off.

I definitely feel my best self when I've had time off, I feel
refreshed and motivated. I'm full of ideas and am ready to
solve new problems. It's simply not possible to give 100 per
cent all the time.

THE POWER OF TAKING BREAKS

- Taking breaks boosts our creativity.
- Stepping away from a project and turning your attention to
  another one that requires a different skill or way of using
  your brain makes you better at your job.
- Brief diversions from a task can dramatically improve
  someone's ability to focus on that task for extended periods
  of time.[23]
- Mindfulness expert Andy Puddicombe advocates the trans-
  formative power of taking ten minutes to do absolutely
  nothing. Harder than it sounds, but so worth it.

EMBRACE SLOW-LIVING

'Slow-living' feels like a buzzword but it's so much more than
that, it's a movement and – you guessed it – a slow one. Slow-
living is essentially about taking a slower approach to aspects of
everyday life. It's about embracing a lifestyle that is the opposite
to the fast culture we're accustomed to: slow communication,

slow food, slow fashion, slow life. It's a lifestyle that is quite difficult to practise due to the nature of the world we now live in, where a news story breaks on social media before it is verified and information spreads like wildfire.

I asked the renowned photographer and popular Instagrammer Sara Tasker for her thoughts on slow-living. She has amassed a huge following of hundreds of thousands for displaying her life through a slow-life lens. Her Instagram account @me_and_orla is relaxing to look at, it's the opposite of face-paced life, it's celebrating the quiet moments. She said:

> I see slow-living as the antidote to the glorification of 'busyness'. It's doing things the hard way sometimes – walking not driving, sweeping not hoovering, or just watching the rain on the window instead of checking our phones – as a way to be mindful and stop rushing ahead. The Internet is great for connecting with others around us, but we still need these moments of quietness to connect to ourselves and to the great history of humans who also walked, swept and watched the rain sometimes. In a world that equates productivity with worthiness, doing things the slow way can be a rebellious act.

TIPS FOR INCORPORATING ASPECTS OF SLOW-LIVING INTO YOUR LIFE

- If you find yourself refreshing/scrolling/in zombie mode, become aware of it. Close your eyes and stop for a moment. Become aware of these moments and stop yourself from being vacantly transfixed.

- Take just a small moment for yourself each morning. Lie in bed for a few minutes doing nothing before grabbing your phone to scroll through Instagram.
- Embrace a bored moment – allow yourself to be bored one afternoon.
- Leave the house early and walk to your meeting or meet-up with friends.
- Watch a film at home, go for dinner and put your phone in a drawer.
- Journaling. Identify and write down if you see something online that makes you feel less than or overly jealous or miserable. These are what Comparison Coach Lucy Sheridan calls your 'comparison triggers'.
- Be properly present at meal times (and when you're cooking and eating).
- Listen to podcasts instead of checking your emails on the commute.

The first challenge is working out our own personal boundaries and deciding what's feasible, the second is having our employers set boundaries by example and third it's all about *owning* our choices and maintaining the balance.

It's time we slowed down and looked up a bit more. Small steps are better than nothing.

CHAPTER 6

The Work-Life Blend

Is blending your work life and home life together good or bad? Not an easy or straightforward question to answer. On the one hand, blending the two means you can lead more of a balanced life because separating the two is difficult to do anyway nowadays. Maybe you blend your work and home life already by working from home some days, working unconventional office hours, doing your laundry in between emails, picking up a family member in the afternoon, splitting up your day however you please and having more flexibility on a micro level. This sounds great in many ways, having that flexibility to shape work around your life and not the other way around. We have the technology that allows us to be more flexible and to have a working life that can suit our individual needs and personal lives. But, on the other hand, it can be dangerous because you can overwork yourself without clear boundaries between work and rest. I'm a fan of the blended approach when done in a way that works for you. I think it is increasingly inevitable that we will blend work and home life more. According to a report this year from FlexJobs and Global Workplace Analytics, there's been a 115 per cent increase in people who work, at least in some part, from home since 2005 in the US – jumping from 1.8 million to 3.9 million.[1]

We have the tools to make a blended life work. However, we don't want to draw the short straw and end up blending our lives for not much professional gain. I'm interested in how we tackle it, manage it, stay sane and be in control of how much we blend our lives and why.

Blurred Lines

Right now, we are merging way more than we think. There are countless people who argue that blending work and home life is very bad and they would prefer to keep the two entirely separate, but they write emails on the way into work on the train. The very nature of having a portable phone means you are already blurring the lines. Perhaps you are checking Twitter at the weekend with the aim of recruiting some new followers for the business. Is this play (because you might be live-tweeting some funny one-liners from *Bake Off*) or work (because you are attracting new followers)? Even if you don't have a flexible set-up, if you reply to an email on the way to work on the train or you quickly check something work-related while sat on the sofa watching *X Factor*, you are technically blurring your work and home life, probably without realising. Since the advent of technology it's become increasingly harder to make work and home life completely separate. It's not that simple any more. And it's actually a pretty new problem. The idea of opting to have work emails on your phone is a newish thing.

Twitter UK MD Bruce Daisley said in a *Times* interview that, 'Since the advent of email on mobile phones enabled us to check our inboxes continually, the working day has increased from seven and a half hours to nine and a half.'[2] This suggests that the blend is making us work more without any extra pay (unless you are self-employed or have a strict hourly fee payment). We just sit back and accept that work will bleed into our home life. It doesn't seem fair.

Work and Life

Work can seep into our personal spaces without us inviting it in. For example, if our partner or best friend is having a horrible time at work it can impact on the way we think about our own job and we can affect their relationship with their work too.

A German study by Hahn and Dormann of 114 couples who both earned a livelihood found that 'one person's after-hours psychological detachment from work was associated with their partner's own detachment from their work. There was a big correlation between the couple's feelings and emotions to do with work, suggesting that we are impressionable and we take on other people's feelings. If your other half finds it easy to switch off when they get home, then you will probably find it easier too, which is beneficial for your family and work life.'[3]

This, to me, is another example of the myth that we can truly separate our work and our home life. They have always interwoven and intertwined in some way, they have always been connected and to think you can slice it down the middle is naive.

If you need to rant about work woes or your boss, go for a walk, go out for food or take a stroll to the shops to talk about it with a friend or partner. This helps you get it out of your system and means you aren't letting negative work energy into your living room. The blend of work *energy* is something to keep a close eye on.

We've never been able to totally switch off from work but we can find the tools to help us do this and we can try to find ways to make work less stressful and overwhelming. By having multiple hyphens to your career you never feel totally indebted to one thing because your time is spread between multiple projects. Project deadlines have shorter windows because you have multiple jobs and therefore the feeling of dread is often not as strong. You know that soon you'll be on to the next thing with a fresh start and new sense of energy. A lot of my work dread came from feeling permanently attached to something and I felt trapped.

When I worked in social media, tweeting for big brands and national magazines, I never ever switched off. I wasn't a nurse on call, but I treated my shallow marketing job like it was the most important thing in the world. Being young in a new job is scary. You feel like you should always be 'on'. Learning to have boundaries is not something you are born with. Part of my role was to keep myself updated across all of the brands' social-media channels, monitoring positive comments, negative comments and crisis-management scenarios (aka someone saying something highly damaging about the company). I would have to flag these damaging comments to the CEO and we'd decide as a team how best to deal with them. I felt on edge *all* the time. No one teaches you how to deal with this 'always on' mentality when you are at school. I grew up convinced that work and time off are totally separate, something you can close the door on, but for so many of us work can seep into all areas of our lives and we can feel overwhelmed very quickly. This might be because work has changed so much since our parents' generation, we were imagining our futures looking so different to how they look now.

My work-life blend was really unhealthy. I couldn't tell the difference between work and home life because the phone in my pocket kept buzzing. I'd be in the countryside at my nephew's birthday party, bouncing up and down on a see-saw or jumping in a ball pit and my phone would go off. 'There's an issue that needs handling right this moment' the email subject line would read and I would feel a metaphorical punch in the stomach as I ran outside to deal with the urgent issue and miss out on special moments with my family. I had to ask myself then, *Is this really what I want my career to look like? Isn't it only going to get worse?*

The thing is, you don't have to work in social media or have a job like the one I just described to have that gut-punch feeling when you're off work and something urgent comes up. Most of us have been emailed at midnight by a frantic boss who expects a reply. To be contactable at all times makes us anxious. I've been in many work environments where the busier you are, the later you work and the more visible you are in the team's inboxes means you are considered the better employee. But this isn't true. Learning what is genuinely urgent and what is masquerading as being urgent is a skill in itself.

Arguably we are working more than we think. If you have a public Instagram or Twitter account, you are (perhaps without realising) promoting yourself and your brand to the world and you are 'on'. The lines are more blurry than we think. Because my work-life blur was so bad when I worked at corporations, I realised that if there was going to be such a blur, I would do it on my own terms. I would treat it as investing in myself and whatever the outcome I would get all the rewards, not the company. It wasn't necessarily flipping the bird to 'the man' but if I was going to be 'always on' in this tech-obsessed, status-obsessed, ratings-obsessed world, I was going to do it my way. I would treat every click, hour, late night, blurred line as an investment in myself and the projects I would one day run. It was my way of justifying the work overload but at least I would have something to always fall back on – my own personal brands and skills.

I want to talk about the pros and cons and how to handle this work-life blend because I think it is crucial to the future of work conversation. I think we are going to be blending our lives more, not less, in the future. Instead of dreaming of the old days, I believe we have to move forward and learn how to deal with the blend. I think of it in the same way as when I was a teenager with a Nokia 3210. No one could really disturb me except for a simple text every now and again. It was normal not to have signal or for my phone to be off. Now I have an iPhone there is no excuse not to reply immediately. If someone doesn't get a reply within thirty minutes they often feel that it's okay to follow up with 'Did you get this? Just a gentle reminder.' There's nothing gentle about nudging an email less than an hour after it's been sent. And don't get me started on read notifications. Instead of the broken old Nokia, we have all-guns-blazing smartphones and the expectations have risen. People dream of the 'separation' of work, but that was back when you literally couldn't get hold of your colleague unless you sent a letter or sent Hedwig over to deliver something. Technology has changed everything and it's here to stay.

Will Self said something which made me shout 'OOOOF' at my laptop recently. We think work and leisure are separate entities, but they are not: 'The idea of not-working and working are locked into an unholy and reciprocal relationship with each other. The fact that you're not working is only because you've been working, and the fact that you're working is only so you can not work.'[4] We work so we can have time off. Time off only exists when we have work. Aristotle said: 'We work to have leisure, on which happiness depends.' Why can't we merge the two and have some leisure time while we work? Why does it have to be two total extremes? It ties into this myth that we will only be happy when we retire or reach that career nirvana we've all been striving for, but surely we should try and have some fun along the way too.

Workin' Nine-to-Five (Or Another Variation of That)

In 1969, Charles Bukowski famously wrote a letter to his publisher John Martin and spoke of his elation at being able to escape his full-time job.

It's never 9 to 5, there's no free lunch break at those places, in fact, at many of them in order to keep your job you don't take lunch. Then there's overtime and the books never seem to get the overtime right and if you complain about that, there's another sucker to take your place.

A nine-to-five has never been a nine-to-five and technology has made 'overtime' even worse.

With the Multi-Hyphen Method, instead of five days of solid work and two days of solid fun, each day can level out a bit and the lines can merge more successfully. I've been able to make up my own work-week rules and my own weekend rules. This is not to say that every day or week is perfect. But I wanted to even out the two extremes of work and fun. Some weeks I might work six days, some weeks I might work three. Some weeks I might have a lie-in, some weeks I might be up at 6 a.m. to travel. It's a totally different way of looking at the working week and it is up to you how much you want to work and not work. It's up to you to plan ahead and avoid under-working and overworking depending on the projects you take on. I used to be miserable all through the week with only a slight bit of sunshine and happiness on the weekend. I used to feel euphoric on Friday evenings and then get the Sunday doom at lunchtime on a Sunday. I wanted to change this so I could attempt to have more balance between my work and rest. I didn't want to live for the weekend any more. This is not to say I don't have bad days. Life is life. Work is work. But I am more likely to have a good day off and a good day at work now.

Perhaps the question isn't 'Is the work-life blend bad?' but 'How *much* are we blending and where's the line?' We need to make sure we are blending in a productive way and not just because we *can*.

THREE WAYS TO AVOID BLENDING TOO MUCH

1. **Even if you're not in an office, set office hours:** Having a multi-hyphenate job enables flexibility, but you still need office hours or parameters. Make sure you set yourself a time frame of working and if it spills over slightly that's okay, but you need to have some sense of when to put your laptop away, otherwise you'll carry on working and it'll feel never-ending.

2. **Have a social-media-free lunch break:** This applies to any work set-up. Have a complete break in the middle of the day – a break from work and social media.

3. **Hold yourself accountable to someone else:** If you know that you might skip the lunch, the fresh air, the walk, the break in the day, the evening off, etc. then make plans to see a friend or family member so that you are accountable to someone else. For example, if you hate exercise, if you plan to go to the gym with someone else you will go because you don't want to let your friend down.

Are We Being Nosy, or Helpful?

One question that arises in terms of the Multi-Hyphen Method is how to communicate to your boss that you might have an outside-of-work side-hustle. This happened in a few of my roles. My boss once asked me about my own projects and I could see she was worried that it might be distracting me from my day job. She knew that I was doing other projects, like writing for magazines in the evenings, because she was friends with me on Facebook. She wanted to bring it up, because she didn't understand how I was finding the time to do it. I thought it was strange that she wanted to know, considering I was getting all of my work done. It got to the point where I did have to choose, because the side-projects took on a life of their own. I would have been happy working on my hobby and having my full-time job because I enjoyed it. But this is the exciting thing about side-projects, they can be small and nourishing, but they can also turn into something bigger, by accident or on purpose.

Sometimes, your boss might have an issue with your outside-of-work projects, but I think as the workplace continues to evolve bosses will have to be more open to their employees having portfolio careers or side-projects. It is so much easier to trial an idea or set up a business online that it is to be expected that people are going to explore other options. The web-hosting company GoDaddy did some research in the US and questioned a thousand millennials and a thousand baby boomers about side-hustles. They found that one in two millennials have one and one in four baby boomers.[5] In the last year, Google Trends shows that searches for 'side-hustle' have increased 138 per cent in the UK and 178 per cent in the USA.[6]

As long as the work is getting done and is being done well, it shouldn't be a problem. We shouldn't feel the need to be dedicated to just one job, 24/7.

Our employers are entitled to know where we are at all times within our contracted work hours but I can't help but wonder whether this needs to change and that trust between employer and employees needs to strengthen. This is especially the case if more employees are going to be working flexibly – a level of trust is needed there. I remember once having to tell my male boss in detail about my contraceptive appointment because he needed to know exactly why I kept going to the doctor's because it was disrupting my working day. Why can't we let each other leave the office for personal reasons, believing and knowing that as diligent employees we are getting the job done? There is nothing more important than our health, that's not up for debate. Without our health, we are useless to our employers.

It is hard to tell our colleagues what is going on in our personal lives sometimes. I remember watching American sitcoms and films as a teen and seeing that some of the office-based rom-com characters could take 'personal days'. The 'personal day' means you can dramatically grab your handbag from your desk, shout 'PERSONAL DAY' to your boss – who looks slightly alarmed but not angry – and then leave to go and sort your drama out. I'm sure it's not as easy as running out of the office whenever you feel like it like in the movies, but in America you are given a set of paid personal days. Wouldn't it be amazing if we had these allowances for personal days in the UK (like they do in America)? The umbrella of a 'personal day' means you don't have to go into detail about your personal issue if you don't want to. In this new public, social-media age we know more about our colleagues than we did pre-Internet. We should be more open. An indication that we are starting to get better at being open in the workplace is a tweet that went viral in 2016 by Madalyn Parker, a web developer from a Michigan-based software company who left an out-of-office message for colleagues explaining she needed a break from work to 'focus on her mental health', which was received brilliantly by her boss, Ben Congleton. He praised her as an 'example to us all' in an email that went out to the company about the importance of talking about mental health.[7] A company called Coexist in Bristol made headlines in 2016 when it decided to give employees menstrual leave that would be regarded separately to sick leave. Nike introduced menstrual leave in 2007, so why is it still such a big talking point? I think it highlights the fact that workplaces *still* find it difficult to give employees flexibility on any level. There are many different reasons why women and men need to flex their day up and it shouldn't be a stigma as long as the work gets done.

The Importance of Setting Clear Boundaries

Boundaries are incredibly important, especially if you work from home. According to BizReport, one recent survey on remote workers showed that 38 per cent wake up at some point during the night to check their email.[8] This is not good for anyone. If you reply in the middle of the night, your boss or colleague is getting the hint that it's fine to expect instant replies at crazy times. Just because we can do more with technology and we can be online all the time, doesn't mean we should be. Just because someone emails us doesn't mean we have to reply straightaway. The amount of time that is 'normal' for someone to leave an email without replying is becoming shorter and shorter, because we are expecting more and more of people. Without boundaries we are at the beck and call of our devices. An endless loop of Internetting.

It should be up to us to choose if we want to blend our work into the evenings. It depends on whether you feel forced or not. It's one thing if you want to dip into some work one evening, another if you feel like you might get fired or your boss will hate you if you don't. Again, it is the psychology and emotions behind the blend. Leaders and bosses should lead the way and show that it's possible to have a healthy blend. If your boss is not leading by example, it's very hard to implement your own rules. The Internet has stripped us of our natural physical boundaries. We can be accessed at all times, we are always connected in some way, we know if someone has read something with two ticks of a message, so we need our employers (even if you are your own boss) to enforce some boundaries to follow. The bosses that I had who also had outside-of-work projects or hobbies really improved my mental health in the office because they understood that there's more to life than just the time in the office and would be more forgiving if you asked for a day off.

To some, the idea of flexibility or remote-working means that you could be opening up the possibility for your boss (or colleagues, contacts, etc.) to constantly ask you for stuff in a way that feels more stressful or overbearing. Because you are available online as a desktop icon and not in person, it could feel more intrusive to some rather than if it happened in the office where someone might come over and ask you something face-to-face. This is why no matter your work set-up, you need to determine some hard and soft boundaries. For me, online boundaries are just as important as physical ones.

THREE TOP TIPS FOR SETTING BOUNDARIES

1. **Manage expectation beforehand:** Let your team/ colleagues know that you won't be on WhatsApp or any other messenger for the afternoon, but you will reply as soon as you can.

2. **Put an out-of-office on:** A friendly out-of-office is a great way to ease off emails for an afternoon. You don't have to be on holiday for an out-of-office. I put one on if I'm having a hectic day and it makes me feel less stressed.

3. **Have pre-made answers you can link to:** In your out-of-office you can answer questions in the body of the email. For example: 'If you are getting in contact about X, this person is best'; 'If you're asking about X initiative, I wrote a blog post about it here'. It's almost like an FAQ out-of-office.

HOW MUCH DO YOU LIKE TO BLEND WORK AND PLAY?

Just as work is different for some people, so is downtime. What relaxes you, might not relax someone else. For example, my nephew hates sitting still. If I asked him to sit still in a chair for an afternoon, he would *not* be relaxed in the slightest. Give him a ball to kick around a park and he'd be relaxed in an instant. We are all different. We shouldn't feel like we need to be productive with our downtime. We don't always need to track our meditation like it's a work project or clock our sleep on an app or feel pressured to finish a book. Society is telling us to achieve in every area of our lives, be it work or play. But downtime is personal. Figure out what it looks like for you.

ANSWER THESE QUESTIONS TO WORK OUT
WHAT YOUR BOUNDARIES ARE

- In what situations do you not mind someone emailing you about something work-related?
- Are you always sure what is work and what is play, or can they merge easily?
- What is your hard 'rest' boundary? (Aka it is never okay to do work during this particular time.)
- What is your soft 'rest' boundary? (Aka you wouldn't mind doing *some* work during this particular time. What would the work be, and why?)
- Do fun WhatsApp groups with colleagues count as working to you?
- Do work parties count as work time to you?
- What noises help you work? Music, silence?
- Do you prefer working in big or small groups?
- What personality traits in your colleagues are important to you?

Try to find the common themes from your answers that you can turn into a set of 'rules' that can also help you find the time for your other side-projects or hyphens, for example:

- I will not answer emails after 7 p.m.
- I will not check my emails on the way to work.
- I will put my phone on aeroplane mode during time spent on my side-project.

Get a Work-Life Fit, Not Balance

I remember chatting with Sarah Jackson, the CEO of Working Families, on a panel once and she said that 'work-life balance' often makes us feel guilty because balance is hard to measure and it's different for everyone. Balance for one person might mean having more time for their children, balance for someone else might mean having more holidays, for someone else it might mean more time for their side-projects or hobbies. Instead, Sarah talked about 'work-life fit', which I think feels like a better term to sum up a work-life model.

An entrepreneur on the panel was asked, 'Do you try and get some balance in your life to prepare you for when you might have kids?' The entrepreneur replied, 'How do you know if I want to have kids?'

We often assume that we all want a variation on the same thing, but what works for us, might not work for other people. Your own work-life fit is unique to you.

Work Perks? Time to Spot the Traps

In some cases, employers use flexibility to try and suck you in *more*. They may try and make us feel like they're giving us flexibility, when really they're requiring us to work overtime and all the time. For example, the idea of unlimited holiday, on paper, seems amazing, but it means you are endlessly contactable or you have to make up the time elsewhere and it might be that you are never totally free from the restraints of the company. In 2014 it was reported on the BBC that Richard Branson was going to give all of his employees unlimited holiday at the Virgin Group.[9] It sounds like a brilliant premise and something that on paper totally aligns with an idea in this book about choosing productivity over presenteeism. Branson said: 'We should focus on what people get done, not on how many hours or days worked. Just as we don't have a nine-to-five policy, we don't need a vacation policy.'[9] I liked the sound of it, a lot. However, I also felt like it could have its traps. Aaron McEwan, HR advisory leader at CEB, said that the trap could be that employees don't end up taking much holiday because they feel grateful to the company for their policy or they're worried how it might look to other colleagues: 'the likelihood of people taking more leave just because there's a policy is actually really low.' Ted Livingston, CEO of Kik Messenger said: 'We found "take as much as you want" actually did the reverse—people took less. The dirty little secret is that nobody will take vacation—it's the nobody-takes-vacation policy. We said, "We're going to have a must-take-vacation policy."'[10]

I've never felt comfortable about the idea of sleep pods and other ways to get your employees to spend all their time at work. Some companies, such as some of the social-networking tech giants, were described in the *Guardian* as 'fun palaces instead of offices and offer on-demand massages and you get a company razor scooter in the welcome pack.'[11] It can get more sinister too, Facebook, for example, offering to freeze your eggs for you. Is this empowering or is this a way of trapping you so that you work for them longer and put your life on hold?

Of course, it's a feminist issue too, put very well by Suzanne Moore:

> The structure of the workplace is still not meeting the needs of women, and the culture is not producing men who meet the desires of generations of women who thought they could have it all. So we end up with huge corporations offering female employees the possibility of reproduction at a later date in return for the 'best' years of their lives. This hardly strikes me as a perk. It is a bribe.[12]

I think it's important for us to see how much the workplace is fundamentally broken, that we aren't allowed work and life to blend in a way that means we can thrive in all areas of our lives. It still feels like it's a choice of two extremes. Perhaps we can't have it all, but I think we should be allowed to try and be allowed to work flexibly without the stigma attached to it.

These perks – endless holiday, beers in the fridge, on-site bar, gaming machines – are all means to justify a fifty-plus-hour week, instead of letting their employees have a life outside of work. In my past jobs there were free ski trips, office parties, table tennis. These are all fine if they happen within the confines of the working day, but to offer them so that employees never leave feels quite dark.

In Miya Tokumitsu's book *Do What You Love*, she says that making employees feel like they love their job has also become a euphemism for exploitation. Hiding behind this mantra, employers are able to squeeze even more work out of their employees. This is another example of why it is dangerous to put all your eggs in one career basket.

Taking Your Work Home vs Taking Your Work Stress Home

I recently read something that made me realise that taking 'work' home and taking 'work stress' home are two very different things. An article on girlboss.com stated: 'taking your work home with you in the evening is one thing, but bringing the toxicity of work stress with you can mess up your family life and relationships in a major way.' This is a mental challenge more than anything. There is a difference between bringing actual work home – such as a project that you could perhaps do in your living room – and bringing the stressful environment or feelings of the workplace. Letting any sort of bad vibes into your home from work can be upsetting. I remember being deeply upset on one holiday because of an email I'd received from a colleague. Because that colleague was on Facebook I kept being visually reminded of her existence and the email she'd sent, it really ruined my holiday. We are simply not able to switch off from our workplace feelings. I'm sure 'out of sight, out of mind' used to work before the Internet.

A lot of people fear that working from home, or working in the evenings could lead to burnout and overwhelm which is understandable. But on the other hand, when working on out-of-work projects OR working to your own schedule, there can be positives in working from home, or in the evenings (if you are a night-owl). I have listed the differences below — it's important to distinguish the difference between them.

Taking work home VS taking work stress home

Taking work home	Taking work stress home
Allowing your device (laptop, phone, tablet) to help you do extra pieces of work	Communicating badly with colleagues because it needs an in-person meeting to get to the bottom of it
Being able to connect easily with your colleagues and boss from home	Taking the unresolved issues of the day home that aren't fixable alone
Being able to be productive, while saving money on the commute	Replaying work conversations in your head that didn't go very well
Being in your own space, creating your own environmental setting and boundaries	

However much you think you have separation between your work and leisure life, they are firmly stuck together, rotate together and are very much a whole. We work to have time off and have time off because we work. Work and leisure are the yin and yang of your life, two huge parts of your life. Everyone gets a bit of Sunday-night doom but if it's seriously affecting you, it's time to change up your career. Your blend might not be quite right.

The reason the blended approach suits the Multi-Hyphen Method is because you are able to design your own timings, the start and end points of the week and where you work. Blended approaches can be positive when you are self-employed or working on a side-hustle because you reap the benefits of any extra time working on something. Too much blend when you are working for one employer can end up being exploitative and can lead to burnout because ultimately you are not in control and it is not for your own company's gain. You are blending for someone else's benefit.

TIPS ON ADJUSTING YOUR BLEND

- If you've blended your work week and weekends make sure you give yourself time off, i.e. if you worked on a project on a Sunday night from home, give yourself a break one week-day afternoon – and don't feel guilty about it!
- Always take a day in lieu – even if you work for yourself.
- Take note of your hours so you have a limit and something to stick to. Just because you're blending doesn't mean you should work more hours.
- Make sure you are taking on projects that won't suck your time too much. Have a solid contract in place upfront that clearly outlines how much time you will spend on it.

CHAPTER 7

Multi-Hyphen Method Toolkit

10 WAYS TO LAY YOUR MULTI-HYPHENATE FOUNDATIONS

1. Pinpoint Your Own Unique Blend

The first thing to do is figure out what your new 'job title' is. It might be helpful to look at the multi-hyphenates and their mixes in this book, but ultimately your mix will look different to other people's. If you are mixing and marrying different roles then you will be offering a different kind of CV. Follow the steps below to help you define what your mixture is and how to build confidence around selling yourself as having many different strands.

- Write a list of words you'd like to be described as.
- Write a list of things you'd like to be recognised for or any side-projects you'd like to start or continue. You might find that you have a list of around five different things that could be job titles or separate skills and that's okay.

- Write a list of all the things you are good at. These can be small things, like that you are tidy, or a good host, or good at listening. These are all important, because the things we are good at (however random or varied) can play a role in each of our multi-hyphenate careers. A lot of our skills don't get used when we just have one job.

- Find the common themes in your different skills. You will be surprised that your random clutch of skills will actually make sense when you add them up. They will complement each other in a way you wouldn't have previously thought of. Take the part-time podcast host and part-time chef – the fact that he is good at making something out of all the different ingredients in a DIY recipe to make a meal is a very similar skill to chopping up bits of audio and making a sewn-together piece of audio. The links between your two jobs might not be obvious, but when you dig more deeply they will be revealed.

- Practise referring to yourself out loud in this new way, with your new mix of job titles. You are a rounded person with lots of different strands. Be confident with it. As visiting professor at Cass Business School Stefan Stern says: 'What people *do* is more important than what they are called. So we should probably all lighten up a bit about job titles. The crucial thing is to be able to understand what someone does without referring to a dictionary.'[1]

- Practise what you define your career as in different scenarios. Depending on your environment, different strands of your job will be more relevant than others, especially if your two strands fit in two different industries. The beauty of a multi-hyphenate career is that you can wear different hats, depending on the situation, circumstance or commission.

Top tip: If you have a hard time finding your writing voice (whether you are trying to write website copy, a proposal, writing notes for this part of the toolkit, anything) record yourself speaking in voice-notes on your phone or into a Dictaphone (I recommended a Zoom mic) and transcribe it afterwards. It helps you focus, relax and find your true voice. I find speaking out loud helps me really believe in and manifest what I'm saying.

2. Grow and Maintain a Micro-Audience

Being multi-hyphenate is not about being an 'influencer'. It is about growing an authentic and real audience of people who know you for doing what you do. Whether that's some new followers on LinkedIn who are likely to hire you, or Twitter followers who might invite you to do some work for them, or just simply connecting with like-minded people who may be of benefit to your working life. Or simply to make friends without an agenda. Social media is amazing and each and every one of us gets to grow communities, whether you are eighty-one and connecting with old school friends, or sixteen years old and messaging friends online who are helping you with your homework.

However, there are traps that you can fall into when you have any sort of 'following': becoming complacent and putting too much weight on one platform. What happens if your

Instagram account gets deleted overnight? Or in a few years it's not the platform of choice? Vine was celebrated as being innovative and popular, with Vine stars attracting different projects with companies and brands, then Vine didn't exist any more. Imagine spending years making your Myspace page look amazing, for people to suddenly leave it en masse for Facebook. That happened.

To be a successful multi-hyphenate means getting work and being known. It *doesn't* mean having thousands of followers, known to the masses, being famous. It means being known within your field(s) and industry landscape. It's not about being a #girlboss with millions of loyal followers, it's about having your name above your door, with people knowing what you do and you saying 'Come in, let's work together!' This is your focus group. By asking your micro community (could be fifty people, could be five thousand) you are getting insight from your core demographic in an easy, non-intrusive way.

Growing a micro-audience is really important for your business, but here is the crunch: it has to be real, which is why it's good to aim small. Having a smaller, more engaged audience for your work is important and ideally it would be made up of mostly people who are interested in working with you (aka potential future employers). Numbers don't matter any more. Because who cares if you have one million followers if only a tiny proportion of them care about what you're doing or saying? Newsletters have risen in popularity because of this very reason. Having a thousand people genuinely interested in hearing from you in their inbox is much more powerful than having millions of Instagram followers. Conversion rates are important for the livelihood of a multi-hyphenate in terms of converting your personal brand into new business, engagement and repeat work.

TIPS ON GROWING A MICRO-AUDIENCE

* Listen and respond. Don't treat social media as one big place to broadcast about yourself.
* Ask yourself *WHY am I posting this?* Always have a reason. If you don't, then WhatsApp that picture, post, question to a friend instead.
* 'Authenticity' is an overused word these days, but be human. People can spot if you're trying too hard to be 'real' too, just be as close to your IRL self as possible.
* Arrange small events or meet-ups (in collaboration with like-minded people if you don't want to do it alone). Ask people to bring a friend to widen the net.
* Offer proper value – whether that's opportunities, information, giveaways, tips – always think back to the WHY.
* Start a newsletter. It's always been the best way to have an engaged small community away from the noise of public social-media platforms.
* Quality over quantity in terms of how often you post and number of followers. Don't feel like you need to post every day just for the sake of it.

Confidence-boost tip: You don't need a huge online network to make a huge impact. In Tim Ferriss's *Tribe Of Mentors* book, Tim Urban said: 'If only one in every thousand of them [Internet users] – 0.1 per cent – happens to be a reader, that amounts to over a million people who will absolutely love what you're doing.'[2] I remembered this and I find this quote to be quite uplifting because it proves you don't need a huge percentage of Internet users to be into your thing as even the tiniest fraction can be a lot of people. Tech can be such a good tool if we use it in the right way to connect with the right people. (There's more to come on networking and making connections in Chapter 9).

3. Always Be in Beta Mode

We can no longer plan ahead in the same way when it comes to our careers because of the speed of new advancements, some of which we cannot foresee. We must remain agile, whether we're working on our own, in a small team or a huge business. There is no way you can learn everything in one go or on one internal training course and then be an expert for ever. This section is inspired by Reid Hoffman, founder of Linkedin, who says 'always be in beta' which means to act like you are never really finished. We are all learning when it comes to tech and the new world of work and none of us are going to be able to skip the hard work of continuously learning and rebranding ourselves over the years. In his interview on the future of work with Deloitte, Tom Friedman (*New York Times* columnist) says to 'Never think of yourself as "finished"; otherwise you really will be finished.'[3]

We'll never totally master anything because there's always more to learn, and that's okay. By being in this beta mode you are more likely to pivot or try something new as you are not attached to one thing. If you take this approach to your work it will mean you are also more likely to be an early adopter (a person who starts using a product or technology as soon as it becomes available), which is crucial in getting ahead. If we stagnate and feel like we already know everything there is to know, we are at risk of falling behind. 'How to stay in beta mode' translates to 'how to stay relevant'.

HOW TO STAY IN BETA MODE

- Online courses, webinars and paid-for lessons are crucial for beefing up your CV and learning new skills like video, Photoshop, coding, languages or photography. For example:

  – Khan Academy offers free online courses on just about every subject, including maths, computing, art history, grammar, economics, personal finance and even entrepreneurship.

  – Skillshare is a learning platform that helps you learn new skills that will help you creatively, from photography to coding to Photoshop.

  – Elevate app is like doing workout circuit training for your brain, featuring over forty games that will boost productivity and confidence and improve your skills in reading, concentration, memory, speaking and listening.
- Use your audience to test out new ideas with, as a focus group. Something as easy as doing an Instagram Story Poll (asking your audience to vote) can help inform a small (or big) decision relating to your project or business.
- Being in beta and on your feet doesn't mean feeling like you constantly need to update or overhaul things dramatically all the time. All it takes is small tweaks along the way to keep fresh. For example, beta mode doesn't mean totally redesigning your whole website every few months, but it

does mean having a look at what you could tweak, or what new features/widgets have just been launched that you could easily add. Sign up to design newsletters and keep an eye on your favourite websites and see how they are evolving.

4. Embrace the Age of Personalisation

We are in an era of personalisation. Online recommendations are targeted at us (most of the time it works well until it gets creepy). Our favourite websites remember our passwords, bank details and what we like buying. We curate Pinterest boards. We organise our online lives with as much rigour as our offline lives. If personalisation (whether we like it or not) is happening so quickly online, then why can't we personalise our working lives to the same extent? This is what the Multi-Hyphen Method is about, personalising our work lives, because we should be allowed to. There is no reason why our jobs can't be like a well-cut tailored suit made especially for us to accentuate our best features.

IN WHAT WAYS CAN YOU BEGIN TO PERSONALISE YOUR LIFE?

- Experiment with which environments you work best in.
  - Take the Myers Briggs personality test, which helps indicate how you perceive the world around you and make decisions. Figure out how certain tweaks to your environment or team set-up might affect your working life. For example, if you are more of an introvert it makes sense that

you really need breaks from a busy open-plan office or co-working space and need to find your own quiet den.

- Are there any traits of your current work style that make you feel guilty even though they work really well? Are there ways of embracing them, instead of mentally beating yourself up?

  – For example, I work really well in the later part of the evening. I've always felt guilty about this, but I decided to embrace it as part of *my* routine, I didn't need to beat myself up about it. It's the same with people who aren't morning people. Another example is a friend of mine who has a paper diary for work meetings and doesn't want to convert to an online calendar even though she's been made to feel like she should go digital. Make a list of all the things that work well for you as a personal routine and try embracing them as they are.

5. Be Your Own PR and Marketing Department

What does your front of house look like? Everyone has a shop window and everyone is judged by it. Our shopfront used to be a CV, a piece of A4 paper written in boring Times New Roman. Your first impression used to be the interview itself: a good shirt, a genuine smile and the ability to not ask rubbish questions. Now, our shopfront has totally evolved and transformed, we have the ability to wow someone with a few clicks of the mouse.

Your space on the Internet is your shop window. It's the place where you are being discovered and you can share it with anyone in the world and say 'This is me and this is what I do.' The mistake people often make, though, is broadcasting elements of their professional life that don't need to be shared. If you have just finished a project that you did just straight up for the money and you didn't enjoy it then don't share this. You will attract more work based on what you share so instead make your front of house a list of all the jobs you've done and want do again. Even if you have to include jobs you've worked on in your spare time. Get yourself in a position where your front-facing Internet presence is attracting the type of work you actually want to be doing. In short, you need to get good at PR-ing yourself.

Who do you want to sit next to online? It's important to know who your like-minded competition is. Who do you want to be like on Amazon? Imagine an algorithm where they group together similar people and brands. Write a list of people who you wouldn't mind being grouped with and start building a network of like-minded individuals or people who might be interested in your offering or content. We are more powerful when we join forces, even with those who other people might regard as our competitors. Whenever I am about to embark on a new project, money-making scheme or fun side-hustle I look at the people already working in the space and the audience that I can tap into. By looking at their audience base you can start to get a feel for who you can target as well. Look at the Twitter accounts of those similar to you or ones that feel similar to your vibe or offering and follow their followers. Cross-promote with like-minded people and collaborate to bring new visitors to both projects. For example, collaborate with someone and make two pieces of content and direct each other's audience to each one. For a podcast, you could record an advert that sits on both channels, cross-promoting your content.

Part of being a multi-hyphenate is selling yourself. We are all salespeople at heart. Want to offload a piece of furniture to a neighbour? Want to flog spare tickets on Facebook? Want to get served first at a very busy coffee shop? In all of these scenarios you are using natural selling skills to get what you want. Selling yourself is a daily practice in a world of online noise.

SIX WAYS TO SELL YOURSELF AND YOUR SERVICES ONLINE:

1. Have a media kit. This should include high-res logos, headshots, statistics, background information on you/the company and testimonials.

2. Highlight any events. Are you/your business going to be popping up somewhere in real-life scenarios? If you are hosting any events, workshops or IRL locations, have a separate page for this on your website.

3. Target your work! Experiment with a social-media ad by using the audience filters on Instagram or Facebook (you can target an advert to an audience as broad or as niche as you like, for example 18–21-year-olds, those who live in Manchester, those who like watching *Gogglebox*).

4. Be contactable. Have an email address in a VERY prominent place on your website or social media.

5. Have strong testimonials. Showcase the best things people have said about you open and obviously on your website or online presence.

6. Press! Have a mixture of big household local or national press endorsements to immediately catch someone's eye.

6. You Don't Have to Quit Your Day Job

It's really much better if you are a multi-hyphenate to keep a day job or at least one part-time stream of income that you are used to having. It allows you to experiment with other things risk-free and to decide what sort of other side-hustles you want to create without the added pressure of having to earn money from them straightaway. (I don't get it when career books tell you to quit your job on the first page. Why would anyone advise that? 'Hey you, holding this book! Just quit your job tomorrow. Go on, just quit. It's fine!' It's not fine.)

Quitting our job in an instant is not something that a lot of us can realistically do, unless we live in a house made of gold with money trees growing in the garden. The 'just go for it' mentality that I read about in self-help books is often misplaced. You can't always just go for it. You can't 'reach for the stars' and 'follow your dreams' with reckless abandon. Sometimes you have to wait for the right moment and create a strategy first.

However, asking for more flexibility within your role *is* something you can do and are entitled to do. It is a sacrifice at first, losing out on a day of paid work. However, the benefits are huge: having a day to yourself (self-care) or to start building a side-business which could grow and add a good chunk to your monthly income. Having an extra project or side-hustle teaches you new skills, supplies an extra income and allows you to meet new people – they can empower you to make better choices in your long-term work. You will be keeping your options open in an unpredictable working world. Short-term sacrifices can turn into long-term advantages. It's all about setting yourself up for the risk and having a goal in mind.

WANT TO ASK FOR FLEXIBLE WORKING? HERE'S HOW IT IS ADVISED YOU SHOULD OFFICIALLY ASK

- Put it in writing.
- Put a date on it.
- Describe the change you would like to your working pattern.
- Explain your preferred timings.
- Explain the effect that this change would have on the company.
- State that it is a statutory request.
- State if you have made a request previously.

7. You're a Multi-Hyphenate, *Not* a Multitasker

One of the biggest assumptions about being a multi-hyphenate is that you must flit between projects like a butterfly, never totally landing on one thing, which isn't at all true. You can have multiple jobs, but you still might commit to one for a longer length of time than another. You might have multiple projects or multiple strands, but you can still focus on each one properly (and it's important to). For example, if you're a part-time nurse and a children's author you can't flit between the two. When you are doing one hyphen you are totally concentrating on the task at hand.

We all know that multitasking does not achieve good results. Brigid Schulte in her book *Overwhelmed*, which is all about time pressure and the pressure of business and modern life, said she realised the moment she was on a downward spiral in her work was when having too much on at once: 'I am always behind and always late, with one more thing and one more thing and one more thing to do before rushing out the door.'[4]

I am a fan of the concept of 'deep work', coined by Cal Newport, a professor, scientist and the author of *Deep Work: Rules for Focused Success in a Distracted World*. He argues it is all about the art of concentration and dedication and that it doesn't matter how *long* you work, but how *deep* you work. It takes the pressure off what 'hard work' means to me. Hard work doesn't mean working all the hours God sends you, in fact, a good in-depth thirty minutes with *no* distractions (no iPhone, no Twitter, no nothing) is actually incredibly valuable and you can get a lot done.

Liz Gilbert famously said that she writes her novels in thirty-minute chunks each day. 'Get an egg-timer' is her advice for wannabe novelists. You don't need the perfect setting, a scented candle or a cottage in the countryside – you need thirty uninterrupted minutes. There are handy online tools like Toggl and TimeCamp that track your time and create time sheets for your business and spot where certain projects might be draining your time. The app Freedom stops you from going online for eight hours and SelfControl app allows you to pick certain websites you want to block.

8. Act Micro, Think Macro

The Multi-Hyphen Method is not about short-term fixes, but about strategies and opportunities that will enable you to forge a new path that is more indestructible than a lot of other career plans.

I've realised that to feel consistently 'on the pulse' is a mixture of being part 'nowist' (being good at getting lots done in a short space of time) and part 'futurist' (keeping a close eye on big industry shifts). This doesn't mean knowing exactly where *you'll* be in five years' time (that's now impossible), but it's about looking at what your chosen industry, world, media and society will be doing in five years' time.

This is the key: you need to be looking at the big-picture trends, while *also* thinking about how you will achieve small daily successes. It's about balancing both things. Always think: *Can I achieve something great in the next days, weeks, months while thinking of how the industry is moving forward as a whole?*

We can't predict what we are going to do in five years' time, but we can look at trends and try and be prepared as much as we can. Looking ahead at emerging trends, especially emerging tech trends, doesn't make you nerdy, it is absolutely crucial. One great way to do this is signing up for trend newsletters, such as trendwatching.com, or the Pocket newsletter, which sends you some of the best of the web-tech reads. Make a habit of curating your subscriptions and who you follow so that you are getting useful information directly fed to you. This might mean making different Twitter lists, or bookmarks, or creating a personal and professional feed. It's worth investing time in the outlets you read in order to get the best-quality information without having to filter through other rubbish to get to it.

We don't know what will happen in the future but we can still guess in the meantime, while making sure we are squeezing as much as we can out of each day.

As Entrepreuneur Gary Vaynerchuk said to Tim Ferris in his new book *Tribe of Mentors,* we 'should not care about the next eight years' but the 'next eight days'. Instead of daydreaming about the future, we should try and squeeze as much as we can out of our seconds, minutes, days, because that is what is pushing us towards our own futures.

9. Use Your Energy Wisely

One positive outcome of our modern tech-filled lifestyles is how we can personalise our days and this can have a direct impact on our energy levels. We can start to unpick and figure out what fills our creative tank and what drains it. The power and control lies with us.

As technology author Tom Chatfield says: 'you have limited willpower and limited mental energy'. This is why the old working structure might not be working for you. Our attention spans have changed and the way we work has changed. We need to conserve energy and use it very wisely.

Tony Schwartz, the author of *The Way We're Working Isn't Working*, says that 'human beings are designed to pulse between spending energy and renewing energy.'[5] Take note of what energises you and deflates you. Personalise your schedule. Note down your energy spikes and lows. Computers can work around the clock, but we can't. It's important that we understand more about our bodies, minds and our own personal rhythms.

Work in units of energy and hours. I used to waste so much time when I worked in an office: cups of tea, chatter, someone's dating story, noise, radio on, countless pointless meetings. A workplace study found an average working professional experiences eighty-seven interruptions per day, making it difficult to remain productive and focused for a full day.[6] One thing I learned is that email isn't our friend. We feel productive using it but it is a con and the biggest time-waster ever. But we all have to use it. So here are some tips on how to tackle inbox overwhelm:

- **Multiple inbox folders:** For your multiple projects, have multiple email folders. Label, colour-code, do whatever you need to do to get your emails out of your main inbox. Filtering them into folders means you get them out of sight and that you only reply to the messages that you absolutely need to. It also means your emails have distinctive project folders so nothing gets mixed up.
- **Schedule emails:** There is a difference between looking busy and being productive. Realising I don't have to send emails in real time has changed everything for me. Sending late-night emails makes you look quite frantic and sometimes you might want to get into someone's inbox first thing but have a meeting that clashes. I like to bulk type out my emails and then schedule them for different times depending on what's appropriate. I might reply to an email in front of the TV, but schedule it for the morning. It's also a good tactic if you want to reply to an invitation but don't want to look too keen! Boomerang on Gmail is a good tool, or followup.cc, Streak, or Yesware.
- **Block out solid time in your online calendar:** If you want to escape constant interruptions or meetings, blocking out

chunks of your diary for deep work can help stop anyone stealing away your time or you accidentally booking anything in. For a multi-hyphenate career this is crucial, as you might not always be available for a certain project immediately.

10. Don't Do Stuff for Free

We've covered that whetting an appetite is one part of the strategy – building a micro-following, having a strong SEO and web presence and attracting clients. But there is a difference between 'putting yourself out there' to attract work and 'putting your work out there, for free'. Do not get into the habit of just tweeting, blogging, writing and promoting your company or work without an end goal of what you want to sell online alongside it.

Disclaimer: I've done *a lot* of stuff for free in the past when it came to side-hustling. When I was fresh out of university and just wanted experience, I had an entry-level job, but I also did stuff for free because in most cases I did get *something* in return: networking opportunities, something to add to my CV/portfolio of work that will pay off tenfold later down the line. I know a lot of people whose past unpaid work at the very beginning has definitely been the main factor in later successes.

'Exposure' only *just* scrapes by as a payment when you are fresh on the scene and have pretty much nothing to offer yet. The minute you have any sort of portfolio, 'expo-sure' is laughable and should be banned from your work vocabulary. But how do we know when someone is taking us for a ride?

Most people pay thousands at university to learn about the stuff that will equip us for working life, only to then be faced with debts and everyone expecting them to work for free 'for a bit'. This isn't the way it's supposed to be and is not fair at all. We need to be upfront about how to make having multiple jobs a livelihood, making it work, having cash flow and making sure the services we provide are paid for and paid on time. I never do anything for free unless it is a specific opportunity that might allow me to reach a business goal (that isn't money-orientated). Examples of this could be an event that is full of prospective clients that will be enjoyable or a collaboration that is focused on making change and not-for-profit.

FOUR TIPS ON HOW TO MAKE SURE YOU GET PAID FOR YOUR WORK

1. Get a middleman or woman: It's often worth hiring someone to sit in between you and the client, who can invoice and chase for the payments (like a virtual PA). You then get to stick to the bit you're good at – doing the work! – and avoid getting bogged down in admin.
2. Automation: Services like Zervant allow you to set up recurring invoices to retained clients so you don't have to worry about doing the same repetitive admin every month.
3. Be upfront at the beginning. Make sure your payment policy (how many days, etc.) is clear and in writing. If you can, ask for 50 per cent of the money upfront before you begin the work. Be clear where the work

parameters are and that any extra work would need to be invoiced separately. Also, sometimes it's good to ask about their payment system/process beforehand, just so you know.

4. Don't be afraid to ask for *more*: You're allowed to ask anything! The answer is never personal, just practical. Make sure you up your rates as you go. You might not be working in a traditional company but you should review, promote yourself and give yourself a pay rise! (You'll find more tips on money in Chapter 10).

Interview with Lizzie Penny, Founder and CEO of The Hoxby Collective

Lizzie Penny started a virtual outsourcing agency called The Hoxby Collective. In her words, The Hoxby Collective is 'a global community of freelancers' who get matched up to exciting paid briefs. I wanted to shine a light on a new type of agency that is helping people facilitate their working lives in a new way. Being a multi-hyphenate doesn't mean being or working alone. It just means having the flexibility to choose your own schedule.

Lizzie says, 'The Hoxby Collective is a virtual agency that uses technology to enable people to work flexibly, whenever and wherever they want. I'm a real champion of the idea of having your own work style, and feel talented and ambitious people shouldn't have to compromise their home life or hobbies for their work.'

Emma: In a nutshell, what's the reason you started your virtual outsourcing agency The Hoxby Collective and what is it?

Lizzie: Because of a vision to create a happier, more fulfilled society, which we believed would only be achieved by fundamentally rethinking working practices. We brought together a community of like-minded people who wanted their own work style and as the word spread we found we grew faster than we had imagined we would, and became more global (we now have a presence in thirty countries around the world). We started to find that we were more of a natural fit for outsourcing across multiple functions – of course as it turned out there are people who want to work flexibly in every discipline and at every level! What we do was very much an evolution, but why we do it was very much by design.

Emma: Why do you think we need to discuss futureproofing ourselves in the workplace?

Lizzie: Technology is driving a myriad of changes across both our personal lives and the working world. The implications of this are far-reaching and the distant future we can't currently envisage with any clarity, but we should try to keep up with the short-term changes and understand how they can best work for each of us as individuals as well as the organisations and communities we are a part of. Anyone who doesn't do this is likely to miss out on the chance to live and work in the way that best suits them, as with advances comes the oppor-tunity to really do what you love in the way you want to do it, building flexibility into all aspects of our lives. We also need to create 'prototype' organisations like The Hoxby Collective to illustrate it can work for individuals, for the community as a whole, in order to show that it is a fantastic way to work and excite others that they can do it too.

Emma: Why do you think people are still so judgemental about the idea of flexible working?

Lizzie: I find the number of people who defend the nine-to-five (or more often eight-eight) working day truly staggering. It's a concept that's over two hundred years old and in that time so many things have changed, there has been so much innovation and progress, and yet the way we work hasn't fundamentally changed at all. The thing I find the most frustrating is the culture of presenteeism that remains so prevalent.

Three-quarters of people believe that presenteeism (being visible at their desk, whether working or not) is commonplace in their work environment and yet in the same survey 88 per cent of those working flexibly believe they are more efficient at work, so it makes better sense for business and for peoples' lives to work flexibly, and yet it's still viewed in a derogatory way. Jokes about 'shirking from home' and the negative connotations associated with terms like 'part-timers' are deeply ingrained in cultures and will take time to eliminate, but eliminate them we must if we're to move to a more future-facing way of working.

I am the CEO of an organisation with over four hundred associates and I work three days a week; the fact I work less than part-time and that the days of the week I work change week to week doesn't make me any less good at my job. As a rule people aren't comfortable with change, but in time we have to hope that people will be judged on their output rather than the time they are at a specific desk in a particular office. A meritocracy is really the best way to work on so many fronts.

Emma: How do you encourage other people to look ahead and spot new ways of working and living?

Lizzie: At the time we came up with Hoxby, the trend we were capitalising on was technology not really being optimised in the working world in order to create more meritocratic ways of working. I think the most important two things for people to do in order to see new ways of balancing work and life are, firstly, to keep their eyes open to what is going on around them beyond their immediate lives but broader changes in the world, and secondly, to regularly reflect on their own lives, and their happiness and fulfilment and question whether they truly have the right balance and what they could change in order to make it work better for them. The third thing of course is to have the self-belief and confidence to make the changes in order to achieve that and often that is the hardest step.

Emma: Do you think it's unfair that it's only millennials that seem to be branded as 'side-hustlers' or thriving in a start-up culture?

Lizzie: Yes I think that's completely untrue. The Hoxby Collective is very much a community of entrepreneurs from all corners of the globe, all walks of life and of all ages. Everyone in the community works for themselves and each person has overcome their own challenges in order to do so, and to do what they love in the way that best suits them. If our inspiring community has taught me one thing it's never underestimate the incredible individual stories that lie behind a powerful and united community like ours – and not to generalise about millennials or in any other way. When you start to look around, you find there are self-motivated entrepreneurs everywhere.

Emma: Do these sorts of virtual agencies allow people to live a multi-hyphenate lifestyle?

Lizzie: We've got an awesome mix of multi-hyphenates at Hoxby. I would go so far as to say it's rare to find a Hoxby who only does one thing! We've got a teacher – upholsterer – events organiser – eyelash-extension business owner – digital project manager – team curation manager and a kids' cooking kit entrepreneur – marketing client director, among others. We think that having a breadth of facets to your career fosters different ways of thinking and new ideas from each, and particularly means you can really love what you do.

Summary

Refer back to this toolkit whenever you feel as though you need a push on how to bring some of your new ideas to life, such as which online platform to use as a springboard, how to grow your audience, the importance of your brand online and why you should go for it. The Multi-Hyphen Method is all about reinventing yourself, your workload and staying nimble but it's important to a) remember why you're doing it and b) pinpoint the basic foundations you already have in place and how you can repeat your success each time. It's exciting to have companies like Lizzie's which help connect multi-hyphen-ates to sustained work, by creating a larger network and system where we all get to use our niche and varied skills in ways that best suit us.

CHAPTER 8

The Four Fs: Failure, Feminism, Flexible Working, Feelings

I couldn't write a book about work and personal success and not include a chapter on failure. I personally find failure to be fetishised somewhat in business books. I see Samuel Beckett quotes like 'fail harder, fail better' plastered all over start-up offices. Failure seems to be celebrated all the time. Failure can be important for the life lessons you learn along the way, but it's also not fun, *at all*. When I wrote this chapter I realised four themes kept recurring, sort of by accident. These were: straight-up messing it up, the confidence gap, the challenge of asking for flexi-time, and how our emotions affect our work and work decisions. I sorted these into the four 'Fs': Failure, Feminism, Flexible Working and Feelings. This isn't a book just for women; but when talking about confidence it's hard not to take into account how much the Confident Alpha approach seems to be rewarded and ingrained in our work culture, and that is often something men already have a leg up on. A patriarchal society affects both men and women, men's setbacks in the workplace are a feminist issue too. Paternity leave is important for men yet many workplaces still don't see it as something they should give out generously. And research by men's mental health charity The Campaign Against Living Miserably (CALM) and The Huffington Post UK found that 87% of men wish they could spend more time with their children. 'Bro' and 'lad' culture can be toxic for both men and women. Equality in the workplace will be a win for us all.

We all face failure and setbacks along the way, no matter what our job is. It's no different for multi-hyphenates and as much as I wanted to write about the highs, I couldn't not write about the lows too. Perhaps you're reading this and don't feel like you have a support system when it comes to your career and decision-making. Maybe you're in lots of private Facebook groups but are too scared to write on them because the community feels slightly scary. Maybe you feel like you can't ask your parents for advice because they have a different perception of work and success to you. Maybe you have just made a big U-turn later on in your career and worry about the future. Setbacks and obstacles in work (and life in general) aren't specific to one industry. Feeling like you're treading water, comparing yourself to the person next to you and feeling like you're not using your full potential are the same old issues people have always battled with over the course of their working lives. The same work insecurities affect us all, no matter our background, age or position on the career ladder. Crisis in confidence, especially at work, happens to everyone.

Failure and Fear

Every job, project, promotion or big task creates a fear of failing. This, of course, doesn't magically go away when you live a multi-hyphenate lifestyle. Every job brings along its own challenges. When I interviewed the author and popular poet Laura Dockrill, she said she often worries that by having multiple different projects she'll never end up having 'one full glass of milk' just lots of half-glasses. Author and writer Caroline O'Donoghue says 'I get the vibe off people that I'm sort of a grappling millennial upstart, jack-of-all-trades-ing it because I'm not really good enough to do one thing well.' This is a real fear for twenty-first-century creatives, it feels very untraditional to have multiple jobs, when really, this is simply how the industry is moving and growing. But we still take on other people's fears and opinions of how it seems too greedy or too random to have so many fingers in pies. We have more options now and there's nothing wrong with that. The trick is how to tie them all together.

I've had so many different job titles over my career span so far, some of which impressed other people, others made people scratch their heads. What I realised quite quickly is that job titles aren't really that impressive any more – it's about what you do and why you do it. It's no longer the absolute goal to work for a big organisation or a household name. It's become quite impressive – or at least very intriguing – to start your own project and live by your own rules.

The thing is, the world moves quickly and we adapt quickly. Less than five years ago the job 'social-media manager' was still seen as new and exciting – now it's just the norm.

Facebook claims it's created over 4.5 million jobs, for example.[1] These jobs aren't all people working directly for Facebook, which has eight thousand employees. Facebook say the jobs have been created off the back of the business, for example: social-media marketers, developers and even indirect jobs like people who make Internet equipment. Some people might roll their eyes at these new job titles. Perhaps it is fear of the unknown, or that many people feel the quality of content is going down the drain because of the Internet. But these new roles have quickly integrated themselves into traditional workforces even though we are still experimenting with how best to join them up. Soon it will be hard to remember how we went about things without them. A bit like those computers that took over paperwork.

People love to mock new ways of working. The backlash seems to have already begun on the term and caricature of the roaming 'digital nomad'. We cling on to things from the past because it makes us feel safer. But accepting that people might turn their nose up at your career choices is a small price to pay when you think of how far ahead you will be in the long run.

I definitely mark down my own experiences with fear and failure as learning curves. I let stigma get to me for years before taking on this lifestyle. I had been starting to earn good money from my side-projects (a thriving blog, consultancy via Skype, being invited to conferences and panels all over the world) but other people's opinions of what 'success' and a 'proper job' was really held me back from jumping ship to manage these different projects on my own terms. I still felt like I needed to work for a 'proper company' and have a name badge that meant something. I remember the first panel event

I did where they introduced me talking about my side-projects, they didn't care where my full-time job was, that wasn't the reason I was there.

I remember drawing a little red dot in the corner of my paper diary every time I felt like I could leave and use my time on my own projects as I began to earn the same amount of money outside of the office, on the side. I finished the year with 320 red dots on the pages of that diary. It was only then that I was brave enough to leave my job. I definitely think we shouldn't ever make rash decisions, but if we have something that is working, or starting to work, and we have enough of a safety net, then we should have people around us encouraging us to try it, not telling us we can't do it. We should always feel free to try things, because the worse-case scenario is we can always go back to our old job, or something like it.

Another fear of failure that creeps up on us is the feeling of an overwhelming midlife crisis. Or a quarter-life-crisis. We hit a wall, feeling utterly miserable and think, *Is this really it?* Millennials especially are suffering from the quarter-life crisis. The Cut published a piece by writer Lisa Miller that hit home to many twenty- and thirty-somethings called 'The Ambition Collision': 'Women enter workplaces filled with ambition and optimism and then, by 30 or so, become wise to the ways in which they are stuck'.[2] We buy into the dream of 'having it all' or 'having the dream job' and when we get towards the top we think, is this *it*? That feeling is scary no matter what age you are. Realising that actually there's no pot of gold at the end of the rainbow. This is it. This is just how life is going to be. Lisa says:

> It's as if the women have cleared spaces in their lives for meteoric careers, and then those careers have been less gratifying, or harder won, or more shrunken than they'd imagined. And what's there to fill the space, except more Insta images of female gratification – vacations! cocktails! – that inadequately reflect the lives they lead?

I definitely related to this. You can have all of the 'on-paper' successes – a good salary, a great Instagram feed and some material objects – but you realise soon enough that it can leave you feeling strangely empty.

When I first told people I was writing a book called *The Multi-Hyphen Method*, a few eyebrows raised around me. A few of the responses I got included: 'But the gig economy is a bad thing!', 'Are you teaching people how to be an influencer?' and 'That sounds like more work'. Work is one of those topics that we like to shut down because it's too hard to talk about it with objectivity – we are so *in* the thick of it. But that's what made me all the more inspired to write a book on the intricacies and complexities of it all, instead of writing a clickbait article.

Everyone has an opinion on the #FutureOfWork. Every day a new invention pops up, every day a new 'solution' to our ever-growing digital problems, and yet we have systems in place for working which were invented for a different (Victorian) century. The workplace has been s-l-o-w to change. However, some of us *have* changed and we feel trapped by the confines of the workplace and are unsure of how best to use the Internet to leverage our working lives. It's not just about the big success stories though, most of us are already dabbling in entrepreneurship without even realising it.

Education never stops. We must carry on teaching ourselves new skills. The current school system is out of date when it comes to the modern workplace. We should be discussing privacy, security, social-media etiquette, public shaming, the new jobs market, starting your own business and mental-health tools. If self-employment is on the rise as a whole, then we should teach people about how to save and invest money and how to do taxes. We should teach young people how to keep themselves relevant, curious and interested. If we promise them the moon and the stars, and a pot of gold at the end of a rainbow, then the quarter-life crisis will definitely come knocking.

Feminism and the Confidence Gap

'Success, it turns out, correlates just as closely with confidence as it does with competence. No wonder that women, despite all our progress, are still woefully underrepresented at the highest levels. All of that is the bad news. The good news is that with work, confidence can be acquired. Which means that the confidence gap, in turn, can be closed.' – Katty Kay and Claire Shipman, 'The Confidence Gap', the *Atlantic*[3]

The big talking point when it comes to the workplace right now is the lack of confidence in general to go after what we truly want at work. The world is a scary place and it never feels like there's a good time to take any risks. However, that's the only way to make a change (whether it's a high- or low-level risk). In order to make a change, you have to take that scary first step. When I asked on Twitter: 'Say you have a project or side-hustle you've been meaning to start for ages, what are the roadblocks you are facing?' The answers were nearly *all* about confidence, or lack thereof. One person said: 'Tragic levels of self-confidence, low funds, little knowledge (or few people to ask for advice) and bad management of time.' Another said: 'Self-belief/imposter syndrome.' Another: 'Fear of failing, prioritising, self-doubt.' Another: 'Self-belief, and feeling that it's "been done".' Another: 'Confidence to actually do it, often it's a lovely concept but making it a reality is a much bigger scarier step.' Another: 'Lack of knowledge about where to start – like trying to dive without any water!' And another: 'Lack of confidence, self-loathing.'

There were some other reasons in there – money, as well as lack of energy, time and resources – but mostly the issue was confidence and I was really taken aback by this confidence crisis.

It's really important that we talk about this, because confidence to take risks and take things into your own hands will play a big role in the future of the workplace. As executive career coach Gwendolyn Parkin says, 'The employer or industry will no longer be the centre of your career – you will be.' We will be at the centre of many decisions we make, as more people become consultants and self-employed and we navigate future jobs that haven't been invented yet.

There are other examples of lack of confidence in the working world. Research from monster.co.uk in conjunction with YouGov revealed that there is a career crisis among young female workers, with 71 per cent saying they lack confidence in asking for a pay rise. The findings highlight that men have more IT self-confidence than women with 43 per cent of women describing their computing skills as 'good enough' compared to 35 per cent of men.[4]

The statistics are there and it's clear women on the whole have less confidence than men in the workplace and this is true across different cultures too. A couple of reasons for this lack of confidence are the fact women have not been in the workplace as long and not having as many women in senior positions to look up to. Women are still often pitted against each other too, because historically there were only a few seats at the table for women. From my experience in the workplace I am sad to say I still feel the competitiveness in the air, mainly from other women in my field. I wish it wasn't the case, but it feels like a hangover from the past.

Confidence can't be bought or sold, but we can use measures to try and encourage more risk-taking, especially when it comes to trialling a new idea online.

FIVE THINGS I LIKE TO REMIND MYSELF OF ABOUT CONFIDENCE

1. Most people are checking their own online profiles out more than yours. Most people are thinking about or worrying about themselves most of the time. No one is looking that closely at you.
2. Confidence comes from doing things over and over again. There's no quick and easy fix; keep repeating and learning.
3. Make an inbox folder called 'Nice things' and put complimentary emails in there. Anytime you get imposter syndrome you can refer back to this folder which *proves* you know what you're doing.

4. Say yes to things that scare you and know it will make things easier in the long run.
5. Nerves look and feel *very* similar to excitement. If you're nervous, try and change this feeling into excitement, more confidence will follow.
6. Confidence can look quiet, subtle and introverted. Confidence doesn't always carry a loud booming voice or wear a crisp suit.

The Dirty F Word: Flexible Working

Flexibility is the future of feminism. A little bit of flex would go a really long way. After all, a study by the Equality and Human Rights Commission estimates that approximately fifty-four thousand new mothers are losing their jobs across the UK every year – almost twice the number identified in similar research in 2005.[5] It also unearthed that 10 per cent of women were put off from attending antenatal appointments by their bosses, putting the health of mother and baby at risk.

Being a multi-hyphenate is synonymous with wanting flexibility in your career. You want to work on different projects, regardless of whether you are a parent or not. You might want a day or afternoon off to add in a new hyphen, be it a child or that you want to paint by the sea. So how do you actually go about asking for that?

According to workingfamilies.org (the UK's leading work-life balance organisation), 'Any employee (other than an employee shareholder) with 26 weeks of service with the same employer has the right to make a request to work flexibly; you don't have to be a parent and carer.'[6] It's assumed that flexibility is often stereotyped as something just a mother might ask for, but it's something that fathers want too. According to Pew Research Center, 48 per cent of working fathers say a flexible work schedule is extremely valuable to them.[7]

I wanted to ask Karen Mattison MBE, co-founder and joint CEO of Timewise, her thoughts. In 2016, she put the issue of flexible hiring – flexible working from day one – on the wider agenda with the launch of Hire Me My Way – a national campaign funded by the Big Lottery Fund to grow the flexible jobs market and bring new hope to the millions of skilled flexible workers excluded from the UK's jobs market. Five years ago, she launched the Power Part Time List in the *Financial Times*, a roll call of fifty men and women who work in senior roles on less than five full days. I wanted to ask her about why people still defend the rigid structure of the workplace despite the hard evidence against it.

Emma: So why are people still embarrassed by asking for or having flexibility in their careers?

Karen: Flexible working can often be seen as 'dirty', as it is assumed to be good for employees and bad for business. Which as we know, is simply not true. Flexible working, and in particular part-time working, has long been hampered by a negative branding. Not least in the context of senior part-time working. Because when it comes to the top team, businesses often look for nothing less than total commitment, and they often – not always – believe the best measure of that is the number of hours an executive spends in the office, rather than focus on delivery.

Emma: It appears that this old trope of hours done equalling success hasn't really gone away much.

Karen: From a personal perspective, after struggling in the jobs market myself as a parent, I have devoted the last fifteen years of my career to driving change, and helping more women work flexibly – in part-time roles, flexible shift patterns, or through working from home. But when I first started on this journey, the world of work was a different place. Now, it is time to take a step back and think again. As the world of work already *has* changed and how people work has changed. It's business that needs to catch up.

Emma: It's an interesting point, that people have changed very quickly – the way we live, buy, consume, meet up, eat, travel, date – and it's the businesses that have had to adapt for new needs. And what about the old stigma of flexible working also being something just for parents?

Karen: I believe that the focus on 'making work, work' for women with children, paradoxically, may no longer be the right thing for women. When it comes to the issue of flexible working, for too long it has been viewed as a concession – given to those who somehow can't work in a 'normal' way. When, in fact, if we look at the cold, hard evidence, there are two critical points. Firstly, flexible working is not just good for mothers. It has been proved to be hugely beneficial to businesses – from improving staff productivity, attraction and retention, as well as reducing travel and property costs. Secondly, if we take a wide definition of flexible working – where, when and how much people work – we see that it is not purely the working pattern of choice for women with children. The demand cuts across all ages and genders, across all life stages and for a whole host of reasons. We need to think again. Flexibility is not for the marginalised; it's for the many.

Flexible working shouldn't be seen as a privilege – it should be a worker's right.

I also asked Rachel Mostyn from the Digital Mums group, the founders of #WorkThatWorks, for their thoughts on why people can be quite reluctant to embrace the idea that flexibility could be a perk for everyone:

I think it's human nature to be scared of change. And I get that. We are an extreme example of a flexible working business with a 100 per cent of our team able to work remotely and flexibly. We understand though that you can't just go fully flexible overnight, so what we suggest instead is that businesses dip a toe in the water and see how they might be able to introduce flexible working policies than can benefit both them and their employees, for example trialling one team working flexible hours for a week or another team working from a different location. If you measure on output vs presenteeism (the practice of being present at one's place of work for more hours than is required), I'm confident you'll notice no difference and will in fact see a bigger uplift in productivity. I also think too many businesses still believe that if you can see your employee at a desk then they must be working. My answer to this is always that if you can't trust your employees to work when you can't see them, then you have a bigger issue than flexible working!

Our own personal definitions of success and flexibility aren't 'dirty' ideas.

In a piece for *Campaign* magazine Christina Lemieux (global planning director at Leo Burnett) wrote: 'The word "part-timer" has traditionally been used in a negative way to call out someone for not being fully committed to their job. Speaking as a dedicated part-time worker (and one of the UK's top 50 power part-timers), I'd argue it is time to move on from that perception and appreciate that the support of part-time and flexible working in this industry is not only important, but the way forward.'[8] It's true, there is something sniffed at when you work part-time. Even if it means working the exact same amount, just across multiple disciplines.

Subtle comments can take their toll and also pinpoint the old-fashioned ingrained ways of thinking too. Writer Sirena Bergman said in a series of tweets: 'I hate when people casually ask 'oh are you working today?' as though being self-employed = being a student or something / Were YOU working today or did you spend most of your morning scrolling through BuzzFeed and then go to the pub for 2 hours at lunch?' There are so many stereotypes on both sides. Either you are a freelancer in your pyjamas, or you are working traditionally in an office. Where is the in-between? Where is the space to talk about the working world in all of its ups and downs and nuances?

A *GQ* article written by Jonathan Heaf approached the idea of a multi-hyphenate with a, shall we say, mocking tone: 'On my last trip to LA, I was introduced to a freelance noise architect/nutritional strategist/sand artist. As far as I can work out, none of these things are real jobs – or they certainly shouldn't be.'⁹

Whenever I do events at companies to do with multi-hyphenate careers or the future of work, there will always be someone who will come up to me at the end, looking a little deflated. The questions are always around setbacks they are experiencing: their parents don't support the decision; balancing a full-time job with a side-project; money worries; and needing reassurance that it's a good idea. What's interesting is sometimes I hardly say anything. I listen while they speak at length about their idea, their plan, their resources. It's all there. They are pitching their idea, they aren't asking for advice, they are asking for reassurance or a nod of approval. It's interesting to observe but it highlights the confidence gap – we need more conversations and resources around increasing confidence at the beginning of any project ideation. Most of us suffer from this need for reassurance as this type of working still goes against the status quo. Maybe it's not as intense as Rita in *Sister Act II* running away from her mum to a music competition, but the stigma around flexible work or designing your own career is deep-rooted in traditional work culture.

When I asked Vicki, thirty-two, a PR consultant in Surrey, about what spurs her on, she said: 'I know it's sad that I need to be recognised by others, but it's not just my boss telling me I'm doing a good job, it's my friends and family saying they're proud of me or admiring a cool project that I'm working on.' It's not sad at all, it's human nature to want our parents and friends to be proud of us and tell us we are doing a good job. But is this a reason to hold us back from pursuing many different projects, especially when the workplace is drastically different to when they were our age?

Another myth of working flexibly or the big romanticisation of 'Being our own boss!!!' is that it's not as true as it sounds. You can never totally be your own boss, especially if you live the multi-hyphenate lifestyle. Yes, you can run your own schedule. Yes, you decide what projects you want to take on. Yes, essentially you are your own boss because you have more freedom and autonomy over your schedule. However, you still have bosses! You still have good and bad bosses! The very nature of having clients means that for a long-term or short-term project bosses are still a part of your life. That is the nature of work. It's important we stop romanticising the #BeYourOwnBoss mantra. By definition, work means you often do things you don't want to do with people you don't necessarily want to work with.

The Multi-Hyphen Method offers respite from the traditional, artificially lit office life. But it is not to be confused with the #goals captions you see being perpetuated on Instagram. As a society we have a tendency to take something and take a nicely lit photo of it and turn it into a utopian fantasy. The freelance dream is far from a dream. But having a myriad of different careers that you merge and make work for you is, I think, one of the best options out there right now for a work-life balance. 'Desk porn' is real. Instagram 'workspace porn' is growing. Instead of romanticising 'being your own boss' I think it's about setting up your own ecosystem that allows you maximum flexibility and decision-making.

You've got this.

Q&A WITH ANNA WHITEHOUSE, FOUNDER OF THE #FLEXAPPEAL MOVEMENT

As I hope you've now come to realise, a big part of being a multi-hyphenate is flexibility, being able to chop up your working week into different pieces. Those multiple pieces make up a salary. I spoke to Anna Whitehouse – a writer – blogger – podcaster – campaigner – author – founder of the parenting media hub Mother Pukka – and asked her about her campaign #FlexAppeal. She believes people should have flexibility in their lives in order to reach their full potential in personal and professional realms.

Emma: What was your biggest disappointment when it came to the workplace? What had to change?

Anna: The moment when I realised my employers were not looking at what we were doing but simply where we were sitting. That was when I mentally quit. It seems obvious as an employer that you would focus on output over simply chastising someone for being in at 9.02 a.m.

Emma: What are the biggest challenges you've faced in your #FlexAppeal campaign?

Anna: People thinking it doesn't affect them. The assumption that it's a 'mummy wants to see more of her Weetabix-smattered child' issue. Flexible working is for everyone. We are no longer a generation that simply seeks things (holidays, fat salaries, benefits), we also seek life. We seek a work-life balance and the companies that get that will attract the talent.

Emma: Also, what do you say to naysayer people who say flexibility is bad because it means you could work 24/7 on your phone from anywhere?

Anna: It's about control. It's about controlling how and where you work to the best of your ability. Everyone will do this differently and some will not thrive in this environment. But, then, many don't thrive in the archaic nine-to-five system. I've stopped pretending I'm not a mother at work and I've stopped pretending I'm not working when at home. I am happier, healthier and in combining those two things I'm able to give more to my job. I wrote a *Sunday Times* bestselling book in two months while pregnant and without wanting to be a praise monkey, I want that to be living proof to my previous employers of what can be achieved with a little flex.

Emma: Where do you think the workplace is heading?

Anna: In this digitally savvy world it has to be moving to a more flexible realm. It was Sir Ian McKellen's great-great-grandfather who pioneered the two-day weekend in the 1800s. That's working out okay for us all. It's simply a matter of time.

Feelings and Work Emotion

Julius Caesar famously wept at the feet of a statue of Alexander the Great. 'Do you not think it is matter for sorrow that while Alexander, at my age, was already king of so many peoples, I have as yet achieved no brilliant success?'[10]

Even Caesar compared himself. People have always compared themselves to others. But before the Internet, at least we weren't tuned into other people's every passing thought or life #goals 24/7, now we are constantly ambushed with other people's perfect lives. The onslaught of images makes it hard for us to be happy with what we've got. How do we make sure we are looking after our mental health and not comparing ourselves all the time?

A friend of mine, Lucy Sheridan, is the UK's first ever comparison coach. She guides and coaches people and businesses on how to live comparison-free or at least how to turn down the volume on your inner critic and equally stop being so much of a nosey neighbour. One of my favourite sayings of hers is, 'Don't be somebody else's tribute act'. She also describes the all-singing, all-dancing images on Instagram that we all get quite jealous of as the 'Las Vegas of comparison'. It's such a good description – the Internet really is full of bright lights and rides and loud music and everyone else having a better time on planet earth than you.

Here's my theory: it's harder to compare yourself to others when you are owning your own path, your own set-up, your own hyphens. It's harder to compare when your path and career ladders look so different to other people's. It's harder to compare when there's not one idea of success, or one ladder for all. See people as inspirational rather than a direct comparison. Allow yourself to be inspired by others and learn from them.

Working for yourself or on your own projects can often be a lonely experience at times. It can come as a shock if you are always used to being surrounded by noisy colleagues in a noisy office space. As author Steven Heighton says: 'Now, social media and the internet offer the introvert a poisonous compromise: you can be alone in your room and at the same time connected to others, if more or less on your own terms. Alone, yet not alone.'[11]

It's a serious discussion, considering that Gen Z might find it easy not to leave the house if they can do everything from their laptops. Jean Twenge, an American psychologist, said in a piece in the *Atlantic*: 'Social-networking sites like Facebook promise to connect us to friends. But the portrait of iGen teens emerging from the data is one of a lonely, dislocated generation.'[12] It's true. We shouldn't be conned. We should make sure we are having real connections and relationships.

It's one thing opening up your work life to more flexibility and having a little bit of flex here and there, but this isn't about totally turning your back on some traditional aspects of work. Flexibility is about friends, self-care, family life, having enough time off to avoid burnout, having the occasional afternoon off, or a job-share so you have more time for side-hustles or simply being there at the school gate on time. These are all positive things and can dramatically change a lifestyle. However, it's all about balance. An article in *Harvard Business Review* said that: 'In the workplace, new models of working—such as telecommuting and some on-demand "gig economy" contracting arrangements—have created flexibility but often reduce the opportunities for in-person interaction and relationships.'[13] I want to emphasise the importance of IRL contact. One of the biggest myths is that as a multi-hyphenate, especially when your hyphens are in the digital sphere, you spend all your time online or on your own. Being flexible doesn't have to mean spending all your time on your own or separated from conversations. It's important to keep up connections and not lose out from not physically being in the office 24/7.

I find social media the best way to meet like-minded people – people with whom to share a real-life coffee! Michelle Kennedy launched the Peanut app for mums who want to connect, whether that's messaging someone while at home breastfeeding, or someone to meet up with in person. Twitter, private Facebook groups and Instagram have all facilitated me meeting up with people. (It helps that my job is to interview people too). It's important not to let 'remote working' mean 'too much time alone'. Tech has allowed us to earn money online, but we still need face-to-face interactions and opportunities to meet new people. Automattic – the company behind leading blogging software WordPress – are one of the first companies to adopt a 100 per cent remote workforce. They don't even have an IRL office and stay in contact with employees through their own online message board. This has its benefits, but it can be lonely, or you can spend too much time on your own in general, which can feel a bit weird after a while.

Freelance writer Morgan Jerkins wrote on Twitter: 'Mon-Fri, if I'm not going out to eat with someone, I may only speak a sentence or two to a delivery guy or fitness instructor. I realised this when I started teaching online. My jaw would start hurting and I was like, "Whoa, when's the last time I actually spoke?"' I am grateful for people like Morgan on Twitter for sharing her honest experiences of how we all struggle to keep things balanced, they help us all learn and grow. After all, for so many of us now, the Internet is our office. And it's important we step outside it sometimes, too.

HOW TO BE SOCIAL OUTSIDE OF
TRADITIONAL OFFICE SPACES

* Book in a breakfast meeting first thing so that you start off your day with meeting someone IRL.
* Join a monthly book club so that you are meeting new people in a regular, enjoyable safe space.
* Sign up to Eventbrite alerts for events or networking opportunities local to you on themes that interest you.
* Have a set time in the week dedicated to meetings where you can meet everyone in one go. Try not to agree to coffees sprinkled throughout the day as this can lead to distractions from getting your teeth into projects. Remember, travelling to meetings can burn through a lot of time too, try and use that time wisely while commuting.

- Have your own after-work drinks with other multi-hyphenate friends (same for Christmas parties).

No job or working life is perfect. It would be naive to assume there is a perfect solution for everyone. Any lifestyle takes maintenance, motivation and conquering obstacles along the way. We all have career ups and downs, but on the whole, the benefits of freedom and autonomy can definitely outweigh the negatives.

CHAPTER 9

Real vs Shallow Connections

> 'You have to build your own networks, make friends with people, cross benches, friends on the left, right and middle. It involves lots of cups of tea – no magic. I'm building networks so hopefully when you need them in future you can ask for their support.' – Martha Lane Fox, the *Telegraph*, 2014

A crucial aspect of creating your own career is knowing how to socialise and build connections in a way that works for you, especially if you're a multi-hyphenate. Not everyone is comfortable singing and jazz-hands-ing their way into every social-networking event, in fact, I don't know anyone who enjoys talking to people with a name badge on and holding a glass of slightly warm wine. It's easy to immediately clam up, and it's very hard to be yourself in such contrived scenarios.

However, there's no denying that networking is important. Connecting with new people and being visible online means that the chances of you being seen and potentially employed or commissioned increases. Putting a face to an email address and meeting people in person is *so* important. Also meeting a lot of new people quite regularly and getting out of your same circle is important. Much like the theory of probability. How probable is it that you will get that job/project/deal? The probability lies in how much you are willing to put yourself out there, put yourself in the room and reach out and connect with others. The more people you meet and connect with increases the probability of getting to work with those people. It's a numbers game. I don't believe some people are naturally better at networking or socialising than others, I just think some people enjoy it more.

Whether we like our jobs or not, our work and career become a huge part of our identity. It's one of the first things people ask about to get a sense of who you are, even though it's often not the best question to ask to truly get to know someone. There are a few better leading questions to ask someone to start to get to know them. Each of these questions below allows someone to mention their day job, side-hustle or simply what they enjoy doing with their time without directly asking them 'What do you do for a job?' And yes, I crowdsourced these on Twitter.

THINGS TO ASK INSTEAD OF 'SO, WHAT DO YOU DO?'

- What are you excited about at the moment?
- What are you working on right now?
- What do you like to do?
- How can I check out your work?
- What brings you to this event?
- What's your latest obsession?

- What have you done recently that you're most proud of?
- What are you passionate about?
- What do you do for fun?

It's Not Who You Know, It's Who Knows You

The goal is for people to know you, know of you, know of your work. This isn't an exercise in 'getting famous on the Internet' (that is definitely not the answer) but the more people know of what you (or your company) do the better. It's about being recognised by a small portion of people for doing something well, who might go on to tell others about you and your work. It's exactly the same as having a local business in a tiny town, where everyone knows of you. You would want people to know the sign above your door and tell their friends to come to your shop or local business. It's taking that small-town, trusted approach and applying it to the Internet.

TIPS FOR CONNECTING ONLINE

- Back in the day people would have a little black book of all their contacts, now we have so many different tools. Google Sheets can be a good place to write down names and companies to keep track of people you've met. Twitter lists are useful for different categories of useful contacts.
- Follow up soon after you've met in person. Strike while the iron is hot.
- Try not to breadcrumb (the act of leading someone on by contacting them intermittently – be that by text or social media – to keep them hanging on). Be upfront about if you

have time to meet up, or if you don't. It makes it easier when both parties are honest about time schedules instead of wasting time going back and forth.

- Don't be too sweetly overfamiliar – you're not in best friend territory yet.
- Follow new people regularly. To find new people to follow, who you think might like your work or company, find a similar company/person who you like and see who follows them.
- Be open-minded. Try new apps (business apps like Bumble Bizz have launched to rival LinkedIn), but if they don't work for you, don't force it. If they work for you, great! Experiment and find the platforms that best suit you.
- It's not about the numbers when it comes to having a good, strong network. Having lots of online followers doesn't necessarily mean you have a larger network. Put in the time to grow and nurture micro-communities – in a private group, email thread or regular drinks meet-ups.
- Only get in touch with people when it's truly relevant for both of you. The aim with networking and connecting is to make people's lives easier. Make a mutually beneficial suggestion. Be targeted in everything you do.
- Don't make a habit of straight-up asking people you hardly know for favours. Make an effort to make it worth their while.
- Connect and introduce other people in your network to each other. Do it without an agenda, but those two people will remember you for connecting them. (This can also be done IRL!)

Why You Need to Get Offline to Meet People

> 'I am telling you that the longer you look into that magical window in your phone, the farther you will drift from the heart of who you are.' – Heather Havrilesky, in her 'Ask Polly' column, The Cut

Networking online brings you lots of opportunities and connections and job requests. Of course, yes, sometimes a gem of an email falls into your inbox, because of the probability of it, your name popping up time and time again. Sometimes you do get a magic 'follow' on Twitter that leads to a huge piece of work. But, on the whole, Twitter, Instagram and LinkedIn are also full of non-opportunities, spammy messages and dead connections. It's worth being aware that although they do increase your chances, they're not everything when it comes to making solid, long-term connections with people. True connection takes time and long-term investment without a big agenda. There's nothing wrong with building up your 'numbers', but it's not just about sitting in your bedroom liking, commenting and following people. That is not a long-term career strategy. 'Connecting' behind a screen will never be as powerful as connecting in real life. In order to truly connect, you have to get out there, in the real world, meeting people face-to-face.

One of the biggest myths I'll set out to dispel is that people believe they need to sit behind their laptops 'networking' their way through Twitter lists, using bots and apps and buttons. That's wrong on many levels, but it's mainly wrong to think you can make strong connections by simply pressing 'like' or posting a handful of comments – this is never going to be enough. Any publicist knows the first rule is to put a face to a name – or at the very least to build up a real relationship and to pitch things that would genuinely appeal to the recipient. People you barely know who make such big asks via an out-of-the-blue email don't seem to understand why that will never work. As we are already time-poor as it is, we aren't going to do big favours for strangers. Good work is built on trust and we will always go with someone we trust and have a true connection with over someone we don't know too well. This chapter offers practical advice on how to build meaningful, life-and-work-enhancing relationships. I don't believe in quick wins when it comes to building a network.

IRL NETWORKING DOS AND DON'TS
DO

Be *nice*. It is underrated. We have this idea that being cold might mean that people will think we're powerful and mysterious, but really it will just turn people off from wanting to navigate towards us.

As Caitlin Moran says, 'Just resolve to shine, constantly and steadily, like a warm lamp in the corner, and people will want to move towards you in order to feel happy.'[1] People are attracted to other people who make them feel good, not intimidated.

Memorise your elevator pitch that sums up what you do in a way that isn't long-winded or too brief. Though try not to sound too rehearsed. Be honest.

When you ask someone a question really listen to their response. Don't dart your eyes around the room looking for someone else. As says Jessica Hagy, author of *How to Be*

Interesting, 'If you let other people open up and talk about themselves, you become memorable.'[2]

Organise your own event. You will still meet new people but you will feel in control of the plans for the evening.

Bring a friend who is happy to tag along and be your networking wingman/woman. Help him/her out in return.

Carry simple and clear business cards. As much as people think they're dead, they're not yet. People still use them. Even a bit of card with your email on is easier than fiddling around with Twitter or notes. I love getting home and going through all the cards I've collected in my pocket. (My editor said she was once given a business card with a picture of the person as a child, on a horse, looking grumpy. It worked, as she remembers it, even now!)

Go with your gut instinct. We each read and take on board someone's energy consciously and subconsciously. It's okay if you don't gel with someone.

DON'T

Don't drag on a conversation for longer than it needs to be, whether you connect really well or not at all. Feel free to move around the room. If you need to exit the conversation politely, you can either introduce them to someone else and slip away, ask for a business card or contact details which naturally rounds off the conversation or go and get a drink or food!

Don't get too drunk. Note to self.

Don't say you'll email someone or that you'll be in touch if you're not going to. Take a business card anyway though.

Don't pitch yourself straightaway even if you feel tempted to.

It's Not Always About You

The nature of social media means that we are free to broadcast our lives to others. We talk about ourselves a lot more than we used to. Part of being a mini media house is about having a personal online strategy and mastering your social-media etiquette. However, to truly connect, we can't be shouting about ourselves the whole time. Vanessa Van Edwards says that there are many different types of people in social situations; she calls one of these types 'conversational narcissists' – these are people who hog the conversation and make it all about them. I bet you know someone who fits this mould, who doesn't let you get a word in edgeways. Well, don't be one of these people online either.

Why You Should Quit Hate-Following

There's obviously a difference between connecting and following someone from afar online. Hate-following is a very easy trap to fall into in this day and age. It is the act of following something (Instagram account, website, Twitter feed, blog) and you can't unfollow, even though for some reason they enrage you or make you stew. We might convince ourselves we're networking with someone online who we are really hate-following. Sometimes we may not realise that it is indeed a hate-follow. Maybe you can justify this follow as being interesting or educational in some way, or you must follow for work purposes, but how do you spot whether it's actually not good for you?

Some hate-follows are harmless in the short term, but can infiltrate your mind over time and leave you feeling less motivated or creative. It's time for us to take control of our online environments just like we would with our offline ones. I wouldn't walk into a pub with someone waving a knife outside it, so why would I wander into a hate-forum spewing horrible images? Every time we open the lid of our laptops, or open our iPhone lock-screen first thing in the morning, we are strapping ourselves in for an unknown ride. We don't know what we are going to see. We have no idea. But the best way to look after our mental health and feel more in control is to make sure our feeds are curated to a certain extent, to make sure that we are following each person with intention and for the right reasons. Have a digital clear-out. Know who you are following and why. Maybe you are following a mixture of friends, trusted news sources and people who challenge your thoughts. Be in control of the things you see. But be conscious of whether you're wasting your time online on things that don't inspire you or have any purpose in terms of connection: stop hate-following. Hate-following is an online epidemic.

Monitor how you feel after you've been on social media. Rate your mood out of ten. If you want to improve your mood, have a think about the accounts you follow and which ones might be a secret hate-follow. See if your mood improves over time, experimenting with who you follow and unfollow.

HOW DO YOU KNOW IF SOMEONE IS A HATE-FOLLOW?
• You find yourself looking up their page if you're feeling like you want to vent about something.

- You roll your eyes or feel deflated when you see their images but still find yourself scrolling through them.
- You would actively avoid them in real life.
- It's turned into a checking-without-realising obsession.

Get Outside of Your Filters

Another reason that IRL connections are so important is because they allow interactions to happen without the help of an algorithm. At networking events we are able to meet people at random. Random encounters have been lost a bit when it comes to the Internet because any sort of 'discover' tab on Instagram or social app has been catered and tailored to us based on our previous likes or follows. As Webby's MD Claire Graves says quite rightly, 'Technology changes the way people interact with each other, and some serendipity is lost along the way.'[3] This is not a revelation but it is still really relevant, and we don't have the tools to combat it in an easy way. Everything we search for or click on is not entirely random. My search page will look different to yours, even if we search for the exact same thing.

Back in 2006 a brilliant TED Talk by Eli Pariser called 'Beware Online "Filter bubbles"' was all about how each of our individual Google pages would look different because of what was being catered to us, depending on each of our personal searches. It means that we are not seeing things as organically as we think. Our search engines and feeds are full of ads and paid-for posts and a whole load of behind-the-scenes formulas adapt to what they think we want to see. It's important that we get out of our filter bubble to get new, exciting work. These filter bubbles hold us back when it comes to networking too, we are in danger of going round and round in circles meeting and connecting with the same people. For this reason it is crucial that we get offline to meet people out of our immediate online circles and broaden our horizons. It's important that we get out of our small online bubble so that we can attract some work opportunities to add to our multi-hyphenate work streams. Staying in your bubble means that when you do leave a job or want to move, you will have hardly any contacts outside of your office space. The workflow of a multi-hyphenate is dependent on your solid network and on having authentic connections.

SIX WAYS TO GET OUT OF YOUR FILTER BUBBLE

1. Balance your news, follow a range of different outlets, even ones that don't necessarily reflect the views you hold yourself. Curation websites like AllSides.com try and give you an unbiased look across the spectrum of news outlets.

2. Follow a range of newsletters that include a round-up of articles, you will be able to read what other people have found themselves.

3. Sites like StumbleUpon allow you to, funnily enough, stumble upon different articles and bits of inspiration.

4. Be aware of algorithms that might hide your favourite social-media profiles. Make your own lists to check.

5. Go to events with friends from different industries. Got a friend with a totally different job to you? Go with them to one of their work dos as their guest and vice versa. It

might be a good way to meet new people and tell them about what you do.

6. Supper clubs are a great way to meet new people in the local area. Dinners encourage real conversation and for me they have been the best way of making genuine connections, over and above any drinks event. Meeting new people around a table is one of my favourite things.

How to Turn Your Digital Acquaintances into a Sustainable IRL Support Network

Networking is not about meeting one person who might change your life. It's about meeting lots of different people along the way. It is not about singing 'Someone in the Crowd' like Emma Stone in *La La Land*. It's about making lots of genuine connections over time, having many people root for you while you root for them in return, celebrating others and making some really trusted relationships in the industry you move in. Ann Friedman coined the phrase 'kissing sideways' when it comes to networking (instead of 'kissing up' – an American term for flattering and sucking up to someone). She said that 'the idea that you need an established, well-known person is not always the case. This concept of "kissing sideways" is making a good cohort of colleagues and support [networks] instead of finding one person to bring you up with them . . . I don't think I've ever met anyone important to me at a [networking] happy hour.'[4] So essentially, networking is one of the most important aspects of being a multi-hyphenate – yes, having a good personal brand but a good personal brand means nothing if you don't have good relationships with people.

HOW TO MAINTAIN YOUR NETWORK

- Start a casual Whatsapp group between a group of digital acquaintances who have a common thread. Use it as a way to dip in and out and use it as a judgement-free zone, a place to talk fees, projects, goals.
- Ask questions and open up opportunities for them to ask you questions too. Even if you don't see each other for a while you can still hold a mutually beneficial relationship in messaging apps.
- Whenever the opportunity arises to get someone else hired on a project, let your network of people know in case they want to be involved first.
- Never close off new additions to the network or collective, avoid building a clique.
- Big-up your community online. Use the premise behind Follow Friday and celebrate your favourite contacts online often across social media.
- Set realistic goals regarding your meet-ups. Maybe it's a monthly dinner.
- It doesn't have to always be about work for it to be a good work opportunity. Joining a book club or going to social events can be just as fun and 'networky'.
- Make sure you are efficient with your meet-ups. Never book a coffee in the middle of the day at a place that will take you ages to get to. If it turns out that the coffee meet-up wasn't worth your time you will feel resentful for going. Make sure you always go with an open mind and book in

meet-ups at a time that suits you, so it doesn't matter if anything comes of it or not.

Aim for that Instant 'I Get What You're About' Moment

I honestly believe that a lot of my success has been driven by my ability to connect instantly and sell what I'm about. For example, I've had some incredibly high-profile names on my podcast, but why would they want to come on my show? When I approached Seth Godin (one of the biggest marketers in America), I knew I had to very clearly achieve the following in a short and simple way: a) prove why *my* show was worth going on in the first place; b) explain who I am; and c) ensure he knew exactly what to expect.

I knew I had to pitch it wisely. Rather than just pitching the strongest qualities about me and the show, I tailored my pitch by thinking about what would make me unique and interesting if *I* were Seth Godin and *I* were to receive the unsolicited email. I said that he should come on because my podcast is listened to primarily by young women in their twenties and thirties, which was not his normal audience. I knew I had to give a unique spin on it, else why would he do it? I think it also helps to try and put yourself in someone else's shoes in that moment. If you were them, what would make *you* do it? You have to have conviction in your pitch.

Seth didn't know who I was, I was a total random to him and he'd literally never heard of me before. But he said within two clicks on Google he understood what I did and what I was about and so he said yes. The reason this worked and why Google can be such a strength is that it can show brand consistency. Consistency is really important. It's not about having millions of followers, it's about being clear on what you're trying to achieve and what you have already achieved. It is crucial that your content that is publicly displayed reflects your intentions and who you are.

Nine Ways to Build a Solid Online Presence to Attract More Connections

Building a good reputation in your working life is important, and now that most of our lives are spent online, it matters what people see when they type our name into Google. Of course we all make small mistakes, or write something we wish we hadn't. It's easy for people to unearth comments we made from ten years ago. Curating our online spaces is crucial to feeling in control of your space and how you are presented to the outside world. Here are some lessons learned along the way:

1. AVOID RASH ARGUMENTATIVE TWEETS

Have your digital footprint in mind whenever you want to have an online argument. It's fine to have an opinion (of course!) but just ask yourself quickly: *Do I want this to be accessible online for ever? Will it look bad if I then delete these comments?* Even if it's deleted, it's technically still available somewhere. Plus people like to screengrab things. We live in a fast-paced time of communication, it never hurts to pause for a moment and ask yourself if you really want to be saying these things, or if it might look and feel better if you step away and take a pause. I find that sometimes I get annoyed by something I see, but I write down my thoughts in a journal. I feel better, because I have got my thoughts down on paper and they might inform a piece of content I make at a later date, and I haven't got into a deep spiral of argumentative tweets for no reason. After all, it doesn't solve anything, and only makes you feel worse.

2. CHECK BEFORE YOU POST (DUCKING AUTOCORRECT!)

Again, this fast-paced era of communication means we fire things off left, right and centre. I'm a fan of tools like Grammarly, which help you craft emails with correct grammar and proofreads it for you. We've all had autocorrect nightmares and they aren't the end of the world. But some things are really crucial to get right. Just as it would be important for you to double-check a form you were sending off, checking your public content is just as important. If an error is spotted it can instantly put someone off. It still matters to check things and for things to be presentable even though we live in an emoji era.

3. CREATE YOUR OWN CATALOGUE OF CONTENT

One platform that is working really well for someone else might not be the right one for you. You can't force it and it's worth taking the time to figure out which one helps you best express yourself.

- Do you like making short videos? – Instagram.
- Do you prefer short sentences? – Twitter.

- Are you better at curating other content? – Pinterest.
- Do you want your presence to be minimal and powerful? – Create a static website (some websites are just a great simple design with a basic contact page which can be very inviting and mysterious).

Pick a platform that really allows you to thrive and show your work off, don't sit across eight different social-media apps for the sake of it, it'll be such a waste of your time and could dilute your message.

4. SELF-PROMOTE, BUT HAVE A BALANCE

Self-promotion should always be about getting more work by sharing your piece of work. Always have this in mind. You are sharing your work for a reason, not just for the sake of it. Treat self-promotion as a strategy with an outcome. It will alleviate any moments of *Is this showing off?* If you have a purpose to sharing something (that you're proud of it, want people to employ you off the back of it, or show that you've collaborated with someone who aligns with your views) it will always feel organised and real.

5. INVEST IN YOUR VISUALS

Visuals are really important and if online searches might lead people to your page they will make a decision on whether to work with you based on what they read and see. Words are important but so are striking visuals. Invest in your design, colour palette, headshots and website usability. Visual branding should be a top priority. You could be the best at your job but with an old website that doesn't work you could easily put people off at the first hurdle. I always invest in visuals because I know I will make that money back once I get the work through.

6. HAVE A CLASSY EMAIL ADDRESS

It can be strangely off-putting when you meet someone and look down at their business card and their email address is FluffyChicken69@hotmail.com. Ideally, set up your own domain name.

7. CHECK YOUR PERSONAL PAGES ARE ON PRIVATE

It's becoming the norm to split out your public pages and your private pages so that you are more in control of what can be publicly seen by all versus what you share with your friends and family (this is a good tactic for everyone not just celebrities who want to have private Instagram accounts, of which there are many). That way your public business page can have a clear direction and you can add personal touches to it as and when you want. Even when you achieve your work-life blend, it can be nice to have a space on the Internet that is *just for you.*

8. BUILD UP A GOOD FIRST PAGE OF GOOGLE OVER TIME

Did you know that by opening a new incognito window on Google Chrome (for example) you can see what your page on Google would show without being logged in as yourself and it skewing the results? You can monitor how it looks, what sort of things are pulled in from your social channels – it's good to be aware of how you display to others. Making time to secure good PR coverage about your business is a good strategy in terms of search. If your name or business gets mentioned in good mainstream online magazines it'll most likely show in the first-page search results on Google and make you look good. After all, 75 per cent of people will never scroll past the first page on a Google search.

Making sure you have a solid personal website presence is crucial too, by using keywords, consistency and good design. But knowing what you are wanting to achieve and the purpose of your brand is the first step. No amount of good design is going to help if you don't know the messages you want to get across. Be aware of what photos you upload as your Google Images matter too when people search for you. (This section has reminded me of the creepy online tool called Awesome Baby Name, that allows new parents to choose a name for their child based on website domain availability and SEO. Shudder.)

9. WRITE DOWN WHAT CATCHES *YOUR* EYE WHILE ONLINE

Inspiration on how to fine-tune my online presence in a business sense normally comes from noting what impresses me as I'm surfing online as a consumer or viewer. If something simple catches my eye, or I like the colour of a logo, or a new website widget, or a short video, I make a note of what has stood out on my newsfeed. I'm not saying I straight-up copy anything, but I notice what is working for me as a recipient of the content. Most companies engage in some sort of competitor research and so should you. You are your own audience.

CHAPTER 10

Our Relationship with Money

On Gaby Dunn's podcast *Bad With Money* she asks her guests two questions:

1. What is your favourite sex position?
2. How much money is in your bank account?

Guests answer the first question awkwardly (but usually quite openly), but the second question is met with silence. Which one would you rather answer? Arguably I would feel more naked answering the second one.

I am a recovering bad-with-money person. Sometimes I drift back to my old ways if I'm having a stressful or emotional month. The Internet helped me a lot in overcoming my bad choices and spotting recurring habits. I read websites such as The Financial Diet which gives you true stories and practical advice too. I only recently discovered the terms 'financial health' and what it is to be 'financially literate'. Money is a language and it's also something you need to practice getting good at. I love how blogging and the open nature of social media has made us more likely to discuss our mental and physical health, and I think the last taboo is talking openly about our financial health too.

Our relationship with money is something that affects all of us in different ways: it can create strain on a relationship, can keep us up at night, stress can make us unwell, can affect our motivation and unpredictable circumstances can catch us off guard. Having no money can cause a strain due to worry and suddenly making lots of it can also cause complications in relationships. Being open about your financial health doesn't mean going around telling everyone your salary or being comfortable when people ask you. It's personal. But we can be more open about our struggles, our plans to save and our obstacles in the hope that we can learn a bit more from each other. Making an effort to talk more about money can help us face our fears and specific financial problems.

I couldn't write a book about being a multi-hyphenate without touching on money. It's an extremely important element to all of this and being on top of your finances when you have multiple projects on the go is crucial. Of course you can strategise and aim for a regular monthly income via your hyphens but it is obviously slightly different to a monthly salary from a single source. When you start to work for yourself you have to keep track of and on top of multiple revenue streams. The benefit is you can set yourself up to have a regular cashflow as you have money coming in from multiple sources throughout the month, instead of getting paid in one lump on the last Friday of every month.

I wish I'd learned more about money at school. Taxes, VAT, budgeting – these are all things that I had to figure out the hard way. I thought my student loan was free money, I wasted it on stupid things. I had an overdraft that was never-ending and cost me so much to combat every month. I remember one year spending money I didn't have on a trip to Amsterdam. My mum called me to say I'd been getting letters from my bank, warning me that it was costing me to go into my overdraft so frequently. I broke down in tears – why was I so irresponsible? Why had I booked a holiday when I couldn't afford it? It's like when you're on a "diet" and you end up eating more to sabotage yourself. I would try to save and end up spending more because I would feel so rubbish or have FOMO, which would lead me down a guilt spiral. I would find myself in vicious circles of doom. Many would agree it is embarrassing to be in any sort of debt. It feels like a horrible secret. At the time, when people admitted to being in their overdraft too, the weight started to lift and I managed to make changes, knowing I wasn't alone. It's easier when you have people to talk to. I recently interviewed a brilliant author in her fifties who admitted to still being in her overdraft and it felt so rare to hear such honesty about the realities of money, knowing that life is always going to be full of ups and downs.

It's hard to talk or think about money without there being an emotional reaction. It can bring up vulnerable memories, our worst fears and comparison triggers.

Having Backup

When it comes to work, we give late nights, weekends, we go over and above to impress and improve in pursuit of feeling special and needed by a company in return. We feel part of the gang. Companies sometimes call their employees partners or members as a way to make them feel like they are part of something, when in fact it's a business and you would be expendable if it were necessary to secure the success of the company. The business always comes first. In large corporations you may feel like part of the family but when it really comes down to it, emotions aren't a priority when it comes to business decisions.

Maybe this worry about security subconsciously kept sneaking into my brain, the idea that the world we're in right now is more volatile than before. Evidently having a side-hustle or side-skill isn't just a fun idea, it's becoming a way to stay on your feet. Once upon a time companies might house you, relocate you, help pay for your kids to go to school and genuinely give you things to make sure working at that company for life was desirable. Now, it's different. When big changes happen, and none of us can foresee them until they are coming towards us, it all depends how quickly the changes can be made to the company. Larger companies can be on the back foot when these changes happen and employees are the overhead costs that are often most expendable. Many workplaces themselves are not future-proofing enough and they are becoming overly reactive, instead of proactive. Do your job and do it well, but know that the level of commitment has changed from the way it used to be. We are giving as much dedication as we always have, yet employers can restructure or make people redundant so easily now. Redundancy used to be a rare and very dramatic thing, but now it's happening all the time. This is why it is important to have more than one stream of income. If anything were to happen to your job or workplace, you have something to fall back on. It's about empowering yourself with the tools we have to hand.

Making sure you have some sort of personal cushion is becoming more and more crucial, especially if you are a multi-hyphenate and don't have a traditional pension scheme set-up. One month can look different from the next. One month might be a super-duper money-making month, with many different projects all paying you at the same time, or some big opportunities in terms of sales or commissions coming in at once. You might have months that are less fruitful, so it really matters how you manage your money, save, spread it out and have a real handle on it.

THREE TIPS ON STASHING AWAY WHEN YOU'RE SELF-EMPLOYED

1. Always make sure you are putting away a chunk of income for taxes. Put this into savings (I actually put half aside into a separate account, to be extra safe!).
2. Work out which business expenses are deductible. Check gov.uk for details.
3. Look into getting an accountant – it saves so much stress!

Why Are We So Scared to Talk About Money?

Seven in ten people consider it rude or inappropriate to discuss personal money matters in a social setting, according to a survey by Ally Bank.[1] At a work event recently, someone came up to me and asked me very directly how much money

I make. It wasn't the question that took me aback, it was how direct the question was and how I wasn't expecting it. I don't think anyone had ever asked me so openly before. I ended up giving quite a broad answer that didn't reveal the specifics. I was vague about how it changes from month to month, which is true. It forced me to reflect on why I found it awkward. Surely if I want more honesty around money, I should haven't found it intrusive? Why is it that we find it awkward talking specific numbers? I asked my community on Twitter how they would feel if it happened to them and asked them how much they earn. I received a mix of over two hundred responses.

Sophie Heawood, a journalist, replied saying: 'Personally I find it completely mortifying. Anthropologically it varies massively between cultures but in the one I'm from it's rude.' Music critic Miranda Sawyer then replied: 'I think it depends on who's asking. If it's a younger journalist, I'm happy to be open about how much I earn and what I do/say to get paid.' Heawood then also agreed: 'Oh if it was someone aspiring who needed to know specific rates and how to charge them I would def say. Not a random asking overall income.' And Miranda then totally hit the nail on the head: 'Money is so weird when you live in a capitalist society, totally wrapped up with personal/emotional/social worth instead of just financial.' We want to be open to helping others, but money is wrapped up in so much emotion that it can make us feel so vulnerable.

The UK's top YouTuber Zoe Sugg wrote: '[It] depends who is asking and why they are asking. If I felt a friend in the industry was being swizzled, I'd say what they should be getting, based on what I know from my own earnings etc. But generally, there's never a need to talk about it and a lot of it is just nosiness!'

Karina Brisby said: 'Aussie culture is more open to salaries conversations, learnt that very quickly when I moved to UK.' Writer Kieran Yates said: 'Can't speak for everyone but largely in South Asian communities being asked how much you earn is just par for the course.' So why do we find it so awkward to talk about in the UK?

Becca DP said: 'I have actively been told in the past "do not tell anyone else on the team what your salary is" which felt very grubby.' This has also happened to me. I negotiated a really good salary in a job once and then was told not to tell the others as it would make the other members of the team resent me.

Luiza Sauma said: 'The idea of it being "rude" has been drilled into us by ppl who want to hide their wealth. Secrecy around salaries leads to wage disparity."

So the responses were mixed. Some people were horrified, some raised the point that being transparent meant that people may not get taken advantage of. A female friend of mine accidentally found out what money her (also female) colleague was on – both on the same level – and the difference between the salaries was huge. She was distraught. It's extremely upsetting to know you are getting paid less than someone else. It's hard to know what to ask for when you don't know how much is on the table. This is why discussing money in a social situation can be awkward or tense because no one wants to find out that they are earning less than someone else. Even though I can hand-on-heart say that I don't think money should be synonymous with 'success' (there are definitely times I've felt successful in my work with peanuts in my bank account), there is no denying that making money for something you've worked hard on feels really good. Sending an invoice for a big sum of money feels fantastic! It gives you freedom. It gives you a sense of worth. It shows that your work matters to someone enough that they are willing to invest financially in it. It allows us to make choices. On the one hand, we feel like money doesn't equal success, and on the other hand, it is an indicator of being taken seriously.

Talking about making lots of money is also a tricky one and does depend on the tone. An Instagram photographer and consultant online announced recently that she made £200,000 in one year from her Internet job, sat at her kitchen table in the middle of the countryside. She runs e-courses online and consults on digital growth. Her announcement of this didn't come across as show-off or crass, instead it was honest and inspiring to hear of someone who is based locally and can work for themselves in a niche and thriving industry. It was said to prove a point – these new jobs that are often judged as not being real jobs actually can earn you a very good salary indeed.

Being Open About Money Helps When Asking for More Money

Having a community you can turn to is important when it comes to having a multi-hyphenate career and you need to compare and contrast rates and ask for advice. You can quickly check if your ballpark figure sounds about right or what sort of costs other people have tried for and why. It also means that if you can't take on a piece of work, you can offer it out to someone in your network and the favours end up coming full circle. You end up getting a lot back when you share with others instead of being secretive and keeping things to yourself.

It gives you an added boost of confidence when asking for more money, too. You feel more confident knowing you are asking for the right amount in terms of industry benchmarks.

Cindy Gallop once gave advice to women who might be unsure how much to ask for if they are self-employed or taking on a new job and I always think of it. She said this: 'You should ask for the highest number you can utter without actually bursting out laughing.'[2] Seeing as most people try and bring down your fee anyway, you might as well go in high.

THREE TIPS ON NEGOTIATING A FEE

1. Get the client to offer a fee first, before giving your rate, as their budget might be higher than your set rate.
2. Ask for more – see if there is wiggle room (always worth asking!) and see what added extras you can offer to your service.
3. Don't accept anything too low with the promise of a higher fee next time. There might not be a next project for a long time and you will lose out.

Top tip: If the company or client pays you late, you are allowed to ask for late payment compensation, according to The Late Payment of Commercial Debts (Interest) Act 1998. To figure out how much interest you can charge for a late payment, this is a good resource to use: londonfreelance.org/interest.html.

Why I Started Making Money Unconventionally

'Most millionaires have seven income streams,' according to the business author Manoj Arora.[3] I knew that my fear of being made redundant (after seeing it happen to countless friends) would ultimately mean I would have to set up income streams that I could potentially control. I could see trends in what some of my friends were doing, some across the pond in the US who were monetising blogs, online sites or marketplaces, podcasts, content and their services that could be given digitally. I acknowledged that instead of sitting in one location, working for one company, I could spread myself across multiple projects and have these different streams of income that I've always dreamed about. I could often earn money from four different projects in one week, quadrupling my income. It also suited my personality. I get impatient, am a fast worker, put myself out there and get bored easily. The perfect recipe for juggling multiple projects. I love putting my heart and soul and best self into a project, and then I also enjoy moving on at the end of the project to something else. In my office job I learned how to juggle multiple demands as part of one role all the time – it was my bootcamp. So, I wondered, *What if I could use my time more wisely, using the Internet to do multiple things without needing to waste my time commuting or having endless meetings?*

But there are so many ways to make money online. It's about setting up your own ecosystems of multiple income streams so that the wheels keep turning every day. For example in one month you might be selling tickets for an e-course, invoicing a client for consultancy and making money through

selling a product via an online marketplace. One example is when I told a friend that a lot of people were buying books off the back of my recommendations online. She said I should set up an Amazon Associates account and get a small percentage every time someone buys a book via a link I shared. This is one example of many, but we can monetise way more than we think.

A great resource to see how other people are making it work financially and monetising their side-hustles is the Starling Bank blog. They interview different side-hustlers and ask them how they balance it alongside their job and what their biggest money-management challenge is. For example, Morena Fiore-Kirby, owner of Kodes Accessories: 'It's easy to get carried away investing in new materials and experiments. I always have ideas bouncing around in my head as a crafter, and being my own boss means I can approve any purchase. It's a challenge to keep my feet on the ground and concentrate on what's necessary and viable.'[4] Approving your own costs and keeping track of everything are just two of the challenges. When it comes to tracking, that's where some online tools and apps can come in handy. Examples include Unsplurge, which is an iOS budget app that lets you save for something you love or look forward to, and Clarity Money helps you track the granular details and reminds you to cancel any wasteful subscriptions you forgot about, for example.

There are many different ways to earn more money online as part of a multi-hyphenate career. Here are a few of the main ones.

SEVEN WAYS TO MONETISE A SIDE-HUSTLE

1. Sell your product (whatever it might be) via a service like Shopify.
2. Pitch to a one-off sponsor for the year – essentially an investment from one company for a long-term partnership, as opposed to lots of mini collaborations.
3. Podcasts can be monetised through platforms like Libsyn, Acast and Podbean.
4. Build a newsletter of customers and use it to partner with other companies.
5. Sell an e-book or webinar online.
6. Use affiliated links on social media (for example Amazon Associates), where a purchase made through one of your links earns you a percentage of the purchase.
7. Crowdfund a side-hustle via companies like Kickstarter, Indiegogo or Unbound (if it is a book).

Our Money Goals Are Personal
and All Different

I read something on the The Cut's agony-aunt column 'Money Mom', a column dedicated to helping people out with their money. Someone had written in asking if they will ever have enough money. The Money Mom replied and said 'What does "enough" money mean to you, really? It's subjective, of course, but for most people it involves a measure of independence.'[5] It's so true. What is 'enough' to my friends is strikingly different to what is 'enough' for me. Refinery29 do the incredibly popular 'Money Diaries' feature

which documents the stories of people who earn and spend
totally different amounts of money. The 'Money Mom' question made me ask myself that same thing: *How much do I
want? What is my personal level of enough?* Because my
answer is going to be different to yours. As yours will be
different to mine. Ours will be different to our friends', and
even our family's. Enough is personal, and we should dig
deep and examine how much we truly want.

That's not to say we should squash ourselves down and
think that our 'enough' should be less than we deserve or want
to go after. I remember chatting to Anne Boden, the CEO of the
mobile app Starling Bank, and when asking for a pay rise at
work someone said to Anne: 'But your salary is enough for
you.' What does 'enough for you' mean? Because she's a
woman? Because of her background? Because of where she
grew up? Because of her age? What does that mean? Our
marker of 'enough' should be totally down to us. Knowing
what enough money looks like to us doesn't mean settling, it
means knowing what we want to achieve with that money and
what the limitations on that might be. Having this goal in mind
allows us a way to not compare to others.

Working out how much enough is, in terms of how much
you need in order to live each month, allows us to make future
plans more easily. Knowing exactly how much you need each
month means you know how much you need in the bank if
you wanted a month off to go away or spend time on a new
side-hustle or course. It is empowering to be on top of your
finances and know how much the smallest amount you need to
live on is, and seeing how much you could save by earning
beyond that. Having multiple income streams enables you to

save far more quickly, because although each month can vary, you can also have big spikes.

HOW MUCH DOES MONEY MATTER TO YOU?
* Is a high salary your main motivator?
* What things make you happiest?
* What non-material things make you happy?
* How quickly does the buzz of a new purchase wear off?
* How much do you *need* every month to live the life you want to live?
* How much do you *want* every month to live the life you want to live?

Make Yourself a Very Simple Budget Tracker

Before embarking on a multi-hyphenate work set-up, I had a full-time job and calculated exactly what I needed each month. It enabled me to save any small leftovers each month (knowing I was going to quit and would need some backup) while also having a solid number in mind of what I needed to hit each month when I did work for myself.

* Calculate total income from all different projects = Income 1 (and any income from other side-projects Income 2, 3, 4 etc.).
* Write a list of all your repeat expenses every single month.
* Put your expenses into categories (utilities, transportation, insurance, repayments, misc., etc.) and calculate this total figure per month.

- Calculate your remaining balance = total income − total expenses. This is what you need every month.
- In the rare event that you may have anything leftover, stash it away into savings.

It can feel like a sacrifice at the beginning. You are choosing a new path, freer, more creative. The benefits are huge once you start attracting multiple income streams, but this switch-over phase can feel like you are financially having to maybe go back a step for a short period of time.

Creating Your Own Cushion

The word 'pension' always felt quite alien to me. I moved jobs so many times that I kept rolling it over, losing count of what I'd put in it and felt like it would only truly work if I stayed in the one company who said they'd match however much I put in. It was a good perk, but I knew I wasn't going to stay there very long. I read a tip that said in order to be left with a £30k pension when you're retired, you had to put away £800 every month for the next forty years. Talk about unrelatable and sort of impossible. Who can easily save £800 . . . a month? I decided to use the word 'cushion' instead of 'pension' and started working on multiple projects in order to start making a cushion for my future. According to an article in the *FT*, 'only 16 per cent said they know how much to save to achieve the hoped-for standard of living in retirement.'[6] The 'Bridging the Young Adults Pension Gap' report from YouGov found that 40 per cent of 18–34-year-olds said they have no pension provision, and 27 per cent said they simply didn't understand the system.[7]

A company called Boring Money call people aged twenty-five to thirty-four 'Rebellious Renters': '2 in 3 Rebellious Renters have cash savings and investments under £10,000; 1 in 5 have no cash.'[8] Less than half Rebellious Renters (48 per cent) had a workplace or private pension compared to 71 per cent of Young Home Owners.[5] It's clear that the pension system seems outdated and conversation around alternatives needs to be discussed more openly. If more people are turning to multi-hyphenate lifestyles, we need to start saving and stashing away a pot too, just in a different way.

Our relationship with saving for the future is changing and perhaps it is slightly different depending on what generation you grew up in. Millennials have a different relationship with money to their parents due to the recession and housing crisis. Two-thirds of millennials are struggling with student loans and credit cards (unlike their parents). We are so in debt, that our relationship with money has already been tainted from the get-go. It always feels early to talk about money and our retirement but the earlier we are aware of the importance of it, the better. There will be a time, for all of us, when we want (or need) to stop working.

The conversation involving our future and money needs to change, as the old systems aren't translating well across all generations. It is clear that the conversations around pensions needs to be discussed because the workplace has changed and therefore how we make and save money has changed too. With a rise in self-employment across the board, personal pensions should be discussed way more than they currently are.

Stop Comparing Your Bank Account

In vulnerable moments, I can momentarily get down in the dumps making assumptions about how much money someone else has (usually based on something as woolly as their Instagram feed). Even though money is not number one on my list of what makes me feel successful, I can't help but make occasional judgements and assumptions regarding how much people around me earn, online and offline, from friends to strangers. But the truth is, we don't know how much people are earning, or what's in someone's bank account. Katherine Ormerod, a writer who has a website called Work Work Work, wrote a piece called 'Money's Too Tight To Mention' where she admitted that there was often a clash between what she was showing on Instagram vs what was in her actual bank account: 'Not everything in my life or on Instagram is a free-dinner, but a lot of it is. This so exponentially misrepresents the true picture of my financial situation.'

I have interviewed both high-profile celebrities and 'Internet famous' people with huge online followings who have hardly any money and people with low-paying jobs who have mastered the art of saving. I think a lot of the mystery and taboo around money conversations is because big companies don't want us to talk openly about money. It's a way of keeping us mute, small and under control. We know that having full transparency in an office across the board would cause rifts, awkwardness and cost the companies more money to make sure everyone in the same positions were equally matched. It can be assumed that many pay gaps would be unearthed too, just like the BBC pay gap that came to light between male and female presenters.

In an ideal world we would be fully transparent when it comes to money, because there should be nothing to hide. In the multi-hyphenate world, it is easier to be more transparent about money because you are able to talk about money on a project-by-project basis because it's a different way of earning than one bulk salary. I talk openly about my fees with fellow multi-hyphenates and I know my worth down to the hour. We compare and contrast and discuss rates. I've felt much more empowered charging for my time (instead of an arbitrary number). It makes talking about money easier. For me, it's no longer shrouded in mystery. My salary always felt like something I should keep secret. On the occasions in the past where I haggled for a raise I would be told to keep it to myself because I knew my quieter colleagues hadn't asked. With my work now, which is project-based and rotates frequently, I feel empowered, in control, can talk more openly about it and share learnings from my financial successes without the fear of judgement.

The End (Sort of)

Congrats, you made it to the final chapter! I hope you feel pumped up and ready to spread your multi-hyphenate wings and have a list of notes and actions on how to expand your working portfolio. This is the bit in *most* business or career books where the author gives you a big all-singing-and-dancing conclusion. A big lyrical ending where all loose ends are tied up with a solid 'The End' before you close the book and carry on with your life. Maybe it would include some big predictions too, telling you they are *certain* that one day they would come true. But the whole point of this book is that there is no final nail-in-the-coffin solution to the future of work. We are *in* the change, right now. We don't know exactly where the workplace is going or what our individual futures hold. But what we can do is protect and empower ourselves in the meantime. We can use the tools in our pockets to maintain relevancy, carry on future-proofing ourselves and keep in mind the fact that a lot of jobs are yet to be invented. It's an exciting time for these reasons. We get to reinvent ourselves, learn new skills, pass on new skills, find new, not-so-obvious opportunities and aim to work alongside technology in a way that is helpful to our lives not a burden. We get to work in a way that frees us up and makes use of all our jazzy new technological inventions and multi-faceted human selves and angles. We get to break out of the boxes. We get to quit and start again. Most of the ideas and practical tips I've given you around leading a multi-hyphenate lifestyle are about unpicking the entrenched work beliefs we grew up absorbing and holding as gospel. You might be reading this with some legitimate personal reservations or bones to pick, but this is not about waking up tomorrow and handing in your resignation letter, it is about taking small consistent risks and opening yourself up to opportunities on the side. It's about stepping outside of one defined career box. It's about investing in *yourself*. If you have been thinking about making any changes to your working life, *now is a good time.* The workplace needs to start over again and let go of so many traditions of the past. While big restructures and shifts go on, start your side-project, launch that website, sell your services independently and experiment with what happens. *Now's the time* for us to take matters into our own hands and arm ourselves with our own skills and invest in ourselves once and for all. It really is time to rip up the rule book, get out a new notebook and start somewhere. Which isn't as scary as it sounds. It is more scary to plod along as normal with the rug edging out from under our feet.

On that note, I will now leave you with some lasting reasons why you are missing a trick if you don't branch out and conquer that thing you want to do with your spare or stolen time, or all of your time. I am rooting for you.

It Will Feel Like a Sacrifice at the Beginning

It is normal for something to feel like a bit of a step backward before you go forward. Self-doubt, I've learned, is actually a pretty useful emotion. It niggles at you and wants you to analyse your current situation and *really check* if there's anything you need to change or do. It can trick you too. I read the book *The Power of Negative Emotion* by Todd Kashdan and Robert Biswas-Diener and understood that certain emotions are there to try and guide you. Feeling jealous? It's a sign you want that thing. Feeling full of fear and self-doubt? It's because you might be on to something and scared of how it will pan out. Feeling angry? It might be because it's within reach but you feel like you haven't found the tools yet to really bring your idea to fruition. Behind each of these negative feelings is a sign that you actually could do it. Embrace these icky emotions and find them interesting instead of distracting. You just have to pick off a few layers of the onion to work out how you really feel. Sometimes, things feel rocky, but it doesn't mean it's a bad decision. Once I left my full-time job after years of side-hustling I felt the most vulnerable I've ever felt, but the benefits after months of graft were so worth it in the end. Things take time to bloom. For example, when writing this book, the bits that felt the hardest were the points (ironically) where I knew it was coming together. Let it come together, but it might not be easy at first.

Embrace Your Own Unique Magic Powers

One of the joys of embracing a multi-hyphened world is that you are at the centre and you can bring your (wide-ranging!) unique skills to the table. They might not be the usual extroverted skills that are rewarded highly in big corporations and that's fine. Your own superpowers are probably much more subtle but could bring so much to the table in your multi-hyphenate lifestyle. Are you good with people? Are you fiercely independent? Are you very adaptable and can work from anywhere? Can you learn new things quickly? Are you good at coming up with whacky ideas and have nowhere to put them? Listen to how people compliment you. You have things you are good at, but our current work set-up focuses on the big, loud, brash skills. Keep an eye on the quieter things that will help you get further in the long game and give you an edge over your competition. Remember these skills, nurture them, and know there is a place for them in your multi-hyphened career path.

Reclaim Your Time

As US congresswoman Maxine Waters so famously said: 'I'm reclaiming my time!' Reclaiming your time should be a key factor of work and life today. Time feels like one of the biggest modern-day luxuries but we shouldn't treat flexible working opportunities like a privilege for only a small number of people. It should be more widely available to everyone and a way for individuals to get some time back and burnout less.

Having time – even the smallest amount of extra time – means we are able to grow, learn and be the very best at our jobs. Now's the time to ask and apply for some flexible working, even if it's a couple of hours a week, and push for more companies to offer it as standard. Companies like Timewise advertise flexible jobs, if you need extra time to start on your side-project, learn new skills or take up online training. We also need to make a proper habit of disconnecting from our online worlds more often. How can we be using our time better? In 2014, YouGov found that 57 per cent of British people supported the introduction of a four-day working week. Could we be moving towards this?

Permission Granted

Workplace hierarchies are changing, what we want from work is changing and we don't get our 'permission slip' for our careers from the same places any more. Every time I meet anyone at a work-related event or workshop, 99 per cent of the people who come up to me don't ask me for advice, they ask me for *permission*. They tell me their business plans in detail, they tell me all about the preparation they've already done, the ideas in their head, the steps they want to take, the passion behind it, and all they seem to want is reassurance. This made me realise just how much we are stopping ourselves by simply not giving ourselves the permission to do it. Give yourself the permission to have a go.

Be Open to Change

Change is good. Change can be scary, but change can also be wonderful. Akin and Opinium recently revealed a study looking at a group of society they've called 'changemakers'. You could say this includes multi-hyphenates, a type of person looking for a different lifestyle to the norm and who is open to change. This group of changemakers in the study don't belong to one generation or location, but rather they are 'a group of people defined by their values and attitudes'. It is estimated there are 455 million of 'us' globally, according to Nielsen. You – reading this – you are a changemaker, because otherwise you wouldn't have picked up this book. You are not alone in your quest for a different working life, there are millions of people around us who are looking to make these same changes. Let's find each other. Let's not be afraid to be many different things.

About the Author

Emma Gannon is an author, award-winning blogger and broadcaster and one of *Forbes*' 30 under 30.

She is the former social media editor of British *Glamour* and has been published everywhere from the *Telegraph* to *Teen Vogue*. She recently starred in a national advertising campaign for Microsoft which showcases and celebrates her multi-hyphenate career.

Her incredibly successful podcast 'CTRL, ALT, DELETE' discusses work, social media and careers. It has now reached almost 2 million downloads. It's been recommended by *Wired*, *Esquire*, *Elle*, *Red*, *Marie Claire*, *The Times*, the *London Evening Standard* and many more.

Emma has been a regular guest on BBC Radio 4 on both Woman's Hour and Word of Mouth. She recently delivered a TEDx talk and spoke at the Oxford Union on the topic of social media. She is a judge of the 2018 D&AD New Blood Awards and currently working with the Prince's Trust and Media Trust charities helping young people get jobs, training and education.

This is her second book.

Endnotes

Introduction

1 Carolyn Gregoire, 'You Probably Use Your Smartphone More Than You Think', *Huffington Post* (last updated 5 Nov. 2015), http://www.huffing-tonpost.co.uk/entry/smartphone-usage-estimates_us_5637687de4b063179912dc96

2 Thomas Costello, 'How to pursue your passion and launch a Side Hustle', GoDaddy (10 Apr. 2017), https://uk.godaddy.com/blog/pursue-passion-launch-side-hustle/

3 Ben Chapman, 'UK workers are 27% less productive than German counterparts, say British business leaders', *Independent* (11 July 2017), http://www.independent.co.uk/news/business/news/uk-workers-less-productive-germany-business-france-american-sir-charlie-mayfield-john-lewis-be-the-a7834921.html

4 'You waste a lot of time at work' [infographic], Atlassian (n.d.), https://www.atlassian.com/time-wasting-at-work-infographic

5 Telegraph reporter, 'Workers' after-hours emails cancel out entire annual leave allowance', *Daily Telegraph* (12 Jan. 2016), http://www.telegraph.co.uk/news/newstopics/howaboutthat/12094025/Workers-after-hours-emails-cancel-out-entire-annual-leave-allowance.html

6 Sebastian Mann, 'Nearly 80 per cent of London workers unhappy in their jobs', *Evening Standard* (19 Jan. 2016), https://www.standard.co.uk/news/london/nearly-80-per-cent-of-london-workers-unhappy-in-their-jobs-a3159656.html

7 Chris Stokel-Walker, 'People Start Hating Their Jobs at Age 35', Bloomberg (22 Aug. 2017), https://www.bloomberg.com/news/articles/2017-08-21/people-start-hating-their-jobs-at-age-35

Chapter 1

1 'Oxford Living Dictionary' https://en.oxforddictionaries.com/definition/success

2 Sheryl Sandberg, *Lean In*, London: WH Allen, 2014

3 Kara Melchers, 'Why choose the career ladder when there's a climbing frame?', *It's Nice That* (7 Nov. 2017), https://www.itsnicethat.com/articles/creative-passion-projects-becoming-your-full-time-job-opinion-071117

4 Gemma Askham, 'Forget the career ladder – here's how to get ahead at work (without being a #girlboss)', *Glamour* (4 Sept. 2017), http://www.glamourmagazine.co.uk/article/how-to-get-ahead-at-work

5 Vicki Salemi, '76% of American workers say they get the "Sunday night blues"', Monster (n.d.), https://www.monster.com/career-advice/article/its-time-to-eliminate-sunday-night-blues-0602

6 Mike Russell, 'UK Podcast Statistics', New Media Europe (25 Apr. 2017), https://newmediaeurope.com/uk-podcast-statistics/

7 Elaine Welteroth, (14 Jan. 2018), 'When I moved to New York City . . .', Instagram, https://www.instagram.com/p/Bd76UOXFo1T/?hl=en&taken-by=elainewelteroth

8 Neville Hobson, 'Why the gig economy fits well with the lives of Baby Boomers', Blog, https://www.nevillehobson.com/2017/06/26/gig-economy-baby-boomers/

9 Vicky Spratt, 'Ask An Adult: Why Can't I Concentrate In An Open Plan Office?' (12 April 2016), https://thedebrief.co.uk/news/real-life/ask-adult-cant-concentrate-open-plan-office/

10 William Belk, '58% of high-performance employees say they need more quiet work spaces', CNBC (last updated 16 March 2017), https://www.cnbc.com/2017/03/15/58-of-high-performance-employees-say-they-need-more-quiet-work-spaces.html

11 Paul Robertson, 'Open plan offices are a health and productivity risk – Canada Life', *Cover* (14 May 2014), https://www.covermagazine.co.uk/cover/news/2344756/open-plan-offices-are-a-health-and-productivity-risk-canada-life%20

12 Donna Ballman, 'Late To Work? These Excuses Could Get You Fired', *Huffington Post* (27 Aug. 2012), http://www.huffingtonpost.com/2012/08/27/late-to-work-these-excuse_n_1833155.html

13 Justin McCurry, 'Clocking off: Japan calls time on long-hours work culture', *Guardian* (22 Feb. 2015), https://www.theguardian.com/world/2015/feb/22/japan-long-hours-work-culture-overwork-paid-holiday-law

14 Steve Chao and Liz Gooch, 'The country with the world's worst drink problem', Al Jazeera (7 Feb. 2016), http://www.aljazeera.com/indepth/features/2016/02/country-world-worst-drink-problem-160202120308308.html

15 Natalie Sisson, '[245] The Traditional Workplace Is Coming To An End' [podcast], The Suitcase Entrepreneur (11 Mar. 2016), https://suitcaseentrepreneur.com/traditional-workplace-coming-end/

Chapter 2

1 John Mauldin, 'Generational Chaos Ahead', Mauldin Economics (19 June2016),http://www.mauldineconomics.com/frontlinethoughts/generational-chaos-ahead

2 American Management Association, 'Leading the Four Generations at Work' (accessed 18 April 2018), http://www.amanet.org/training/articles/leading-the-four-generations-at-work.aspx

3 Sally Kane, 'Common Characteristics of the Silent Generation', *The Balance* (updated 16 Oct. 2017), https://www.thebalance.com/workplace-characteristics-silent-generation-2164692

4 'Generation Z', Wikipedia (last edited 28 Feb. 2018), https://en.wikipedia.org/wiki/Generation_Z

5 Pip Wilson, 'Why Technology Is Key To Workplace Diversity', *Huffington Post* (updated 3 Mar. 2018), http://www.huffingtonpost.co.uk/pip-wilson/why-technology-is-key-to-_b_15080720.html

6 'George Orwell', Wikiquote (last edited 8 April 2018), https://en.wikiquote.org/wiki/George_Orwell

7 William Cummings, 'The malignant myth of the Millennial', *USA Today* (11 May 2017), https://www.usatoday.com/story/news/nation/2017/05/11/millennial-myth/100982920/

8 Jared Lindzon, 'The Problem With Generational Stereotypes At Work', *Fast Company* (23 Mar. 2016), https://www.fastcompany.com/3057905/the-problem-with-generational-stereotypes-at-work

9 Rt Hon Esther McVey MP, 'Employers, Need To Wake Up To Urgent Labour Market Challenges', *theHRDIRECTOR* (23 Oct. 2017), https://www.thehrdirector.com/business-news/employment/employers-labour-market-challenges/

10 Chris Smyth, 'Work-shy millennials add to NHS staff pain' *The Times* (14. Dec. 2017), https://www.thetimes.co.uk/article/work-shy-millennials-add-to-nhs-staff-pain-md2cp3ndc

11 Beth Snyder Bulik, 'Boomers – Yes, Boomers – Spend The Most On Tech', *Ad Age* (11 Oct. 2010), http://adage.com/article/digital/consumer-electronics-baby-boomers-spend-tech/146391/

12 Patrick Foster, 'One in four over-65s use social media, after massive rise in "Instagrans"', *Daily Telegraph* (4 Aug 2016), http://www.telegraph.co.uk/news/2016/08/04/one-in-four-over-65s-use-social-media-after-massive-rise-in-inst/

13 Hannah Furness, 'Rise of the "social seniors" as number of over-75s on Facebook doubles', *Daily Telegraph* (14 June 2017), http://www.telegraph.co.uk/news/2017/06/14/rise-social-seniors-number-over-75s-facebook-doubles/

14 Georgina Fuller, 'The generation of slashie employees', AAT Comment (20 Feb 2017), http://www.aatcomment.org.uk/the-generation-of-slashie-employees/

15 Jean M. Twenge, 'Have Smartphones Destroyed a Generation?', *The Atlantic* (3 Aug. 2017), https://www.theatlantic.com/amp/article/534198/

16 2018 Edelman Trust Barometer, https://www.edelman.com/trust-barometer

17 Yuval Noah Harari, 'The meaning of life in a world without work', *Guardian* (8 May 2017), https://www.theguardian.com/technology/2017/may/08/virtual-reality-religion-robots-sapiens-book

18 Bruce Daisley, 'Ease off those emails and smartphones when you're at work, says Twitter boss', *The Times* (29 Sep. 2017), https://www.thetimes.co.uk/article/ease-off-those-emails-and-smartphones-when-youre-at-work-says-twitter-boss-w6dg6kdxg

19 Michael Smolensky and Lynne Lamberg, *The Body Clock Guide to Better Health*, NASW (n.d.), https://www.nasw.org/users/llamberg/larkowl.htm

20 Jonathan Chew, 'Why Millennials Would Take a $7,600 Pay Cut For a New Job', *Fortune* (8 Apr. 2016), fortune.com/2016/04/08/fidelity-millennial-study-career/

21 Rebecca Greenfield, 'The office hierarchy is officially dead', *Sydney Morning Herald* (4 Mar. 2016), http://www.smh.com.au/business/work-place-relations/the-office-hierarchy-is-officially-dead-20160303-gna506.html

22 Aaron Dignan, 'The Org Chart Is Dead', Medium (27 Feb. 2016), https://medium.com/the-ready/the-org-chart-is-dead-e1d76eca9ceo

23 Zainab Mudallal, 'Airbnb will soon be booking more rooms than the world's largest hotel chains', Quartz (20 Jan. 2015), https://qz.com/329735/airbnb-will-soon-be-booking-more-rooms-than-the-worlds-largest-hotel-chains/

24 Emily Ramshaw, 'How Phillip Picardi Landed A Major Magazine Gig By The Age of 25', *Coveteur* (n.d.), http://coveteur.com/2016/08/18/deskside-phillip-picardi-teen-vogue-digital-editorial-director/

25 Ronald Alsop, 'Why bosses won't "like" Generation Z', BBC (5 March 2015), http://www.bbc.com/capital/story/20150304-the-attention-deficit-generation

26 Charlie Kim, 'Maslow's Hierarchy of Needs: Updated', *Huffington Post* (last updated 6 Dec. 2017), https://www.huffingtonpost.com/charlie-kim/maslows-hierarchy-of-need_b_4235665.html

27 Source: The College Board, Trends in Student Aid 2013. Calculations based on average per-student borrowing in 1980 and 2010. http://highline.huffingtonpost.com/articles/en/poor-millennials/

28 Kathleen Davis, 'The Rise of Social Media as a Career (Infographic)', *Entrepreneur* (1 Oct. 2013), https://www.entrepreneur.com/article/228651

29 Cathy Davidson, '65% of Future Jobs Haven't Been Invented Yet? Cathy Davidson Responds to Cathy Davidson and the BBC', HASTAC (31 May 2017), https://www.hastac.org/blogs/cathy-davidson/2017/05/31/65-future-jobs-havent-been-invented-yet-cathy-davidson-responds

30 Kim Cassady, '3 Ways Technology Influences Generational Divides at Work', *Entrepreneur* (29 Mar. 2017), https://www.entrepreneur.com/article/290763

31 Gemma Askham, 'Forget the career ladder – here's how to get ahead at work (without being a #girlboss)', *Glamour* (4 Sept. 2017), http://www.glamourmagazine.co.uk/article/how-to-get-ahead-at-work

32 Randstad and Future Workplace, *Gen Z and Millennials collide at work* [report], (n.d.), http://experts.randstadusa.com/hubfs/Randstad_GenZ_Millennials_Collide_Report.pdf

33 Alina Dizik, 'The next generation of jobs won't be made up of professions', BBC (24 Apr. 2017), http://www.bbc.com/capital/story/20170424-the-next-generation-of-jobs-wont-be-made-up-of-professions

34 Sophie Heawood, 'Interview: Pharrell Williams On Trump's America And His Adidas Collection', *The Sunday Times* (13 Aug. 2017), https://www.thetimes.co.uk/magazine/style/interview-pharrell-williams-on-trump-s-america-and-his-adidas-collection-bxxc02ojp

35 Josh Bersin, 'The Future Of Work: It's Already Here – And Not As Scary As You Think', *Forbes* (21 Sept. 2016), https://www.forbes.com/sites/joshbersin/2016/09/21/the-future-of-work-its-already-here-and-not-as-scary-as-you-think/#2d692e64bf53

36 Olivia Gagan, 'How Generation Rent Is Using Culture & Entertainment To Fight Back', Refinery29 (6 Nov. 2017), http://www.refinery29.uk/2017/11/178425/generation-rent-millennials-tv-film-apartments-flats?utm_source=t.co&utm_medium=uktweet&unique_id=entry_178425

Chapter 3

1 Freddie Harrel, 'About Freddie Harrel' (accessed 18 April 2018), http://freddieharrel.com/about/

2 'The Future of Work is Here: The Skill Economy' [blog], Chase Jarvis (n.d.), http://www.chasejarvis.com/blog/the-future-of-work-is-here-the-skill-economy/

3 *The Future of Work and Death* (2016), directed by Sean Blacknell and Wayne Walsh, http://www.imdb.com/title/tt5142784/

4 Muhammad Yunus, quotation in Reid Hoffman and Ben Casnocha, *The Start-up of You*, London: Random House Business Books 2013 http://www.randomhouse.com/highschool/catalog/display.pperl?isbn=9780307888907&view=excerpt

5 Side Hustle Nation, 'What is a side-hustle?' (13 May 2013) https://www.sidehustlenation.com/what-is-a-side-hustle/

6 Kevin Roose, 'Survey says: 92 percent of software developers are men', Splinter (8 Apr. 2015), https://splinternews.com/survey-says-92-percent-of-software-developers-are-men-1793846921

7 'Caitlin Moran and Alex Kozloff' [video], IAB UK, (14 Nov. 2016), https://www.youtube.com/watch?v=OxoRigaGaZI

8 'Significant number of UK workers "considering setting up a side business"', Thompson Jenner (10 Oct. 2017), https://www.thompson-jenner.co.uk/resources/news/?op=%2Fnews%2Fbusiness-news%2Farchive%2Farticle%2F2017%2FOctober%2Fsignificant-number-of-uk-workers-considering-setting-up-a-side-business

9 Joshua Sophy, 'More Than 1 in 4 Millennials Work a Side Hustle', *Small Business Trends* (20 July 2017), https://smallbiztrends.com/2017/07/millennial-side-hustle-statistics.html

10 Lydia Dishman, 'How The Gig Economy Will Change In 2017', *Fast*

Company (5 Jan. 2017), https://www.fastcompany.com/3066905/how-the-gig-economy-will-change-in-2017

11 Catherine Baab-Muguira, 'Millennials are obsessed with side hustles because they're all we've got', Quartz (23 June 2016), https://qz.com/711773/millennials-are-obsessed-with-side-hustles-because-theyre-all-weve-got/

12 Jayne Robinson can be found on Twitter and Instagram under the handle @JayneKitsch

Chapter 4

1 Mikel E. Belicove, 'A New Study Reveals the Power of First Impressions Online', *Entrepreneur* (14 Mar. 2012), https://www.entrepreneur.com/article/223150

2 Clay Routledge PhD, 'On the Modern Self – An Interview with Will Storr', *Psychology Today* (19 Aug. 2017), https://www.psychologytoday.com/blog/more-mortal/201708/the-modern-self?amp

3 Gwendolyn Parkin, 'How To Work The Workplace At Any Age', *Elle* (1 Nov 2017), https://www.pressreader.com/uk/elle-uk/20171101/284880890738782

4 Elizabeth Segran, 'How Hiding Your True Self At Work Can Hurt Your Career', *Fast Company* (17 Sept. 2015), https://www.fastcompany.com/3051111/how-hiding-your-true-self-at-work-can-hurt-your-career

5 Jennifer Miller, 'Leadership Tips for the Modern Fluid Workforce', InPower Coaching (27 June 2017), https://inpowercoaching.com/leadership-tips-modern-fluid-workforce/

6 Cathy Engelbert and John Hagel, 'Radically open: Tom Friedman on jobs, learning, and the future of work', Deloitte Insights (31 July 2017), https://dupress.deloitte.com/dup-us-en/deloitte-review/issue-21/tom-friedman-interview-jobs-learning-future-of-work.html

7 Kenneth R. Rosen, 'How to Recognize Burnout Before You're Burned Out', *New York Times* (5 Sept. 2017), https://www.nytimes.com/2017/09/05/smarter-living/workplace-burnout-symptoms.html?sl_l=1&sl_rec=editorial&referer=

8 Jackee Holder, 'How Creativity Boosts Your Mental Health and Wellbeing', Welldoing.org (18 Feb 2016), https://welldoing.org/article/how-creativity-boosts-your-mental-health-wellbeing

9 Lydia Ruffles, 'Art and soul: how sparking your creativity helps you stay well', *Guardian* (5 Nov. 2017), https://amp.theguardian.com/lifeandstyle/2017/nov/05/art-and-soul-how-sparking-creativity-helps-you-stay-well

Chapter 5

1 Lisa M. Gerry, '10 Signs You're Burning Out – And What To Do About It', *Forbes* (1 April 2013)

2 Katie Forster, 'Third of UK workers experiencing anxiety, depression or stress, survey finds', *Independent* (6 July 2017), http://www.independent.

co.uk/news/health/uk-workers-depression-stress-anxiety-survey-a7827656.
html

3 Kenneth R. Rosen, 'How to Recognize Burnout Before You're Burned
Out', *New York Times* (5 Sept. 2017), https://www.nytimes.com/2017/09/05/
smarter-living/workplace-burnout-symptoms.html

4 Jacquelyn Smith, 'Here's why workplace stress is costing employers
$300 billion a year', Business Insider (6 June 2016), http://uk.businessinsider.
com/how-stress-at-work-is-costing-employers-300-billion-a-year-
2016-6?r=US&IR=T

5 Peter Fleming, 'Do you work more than 39 hours a week? Your job could
be killing you', *Guardian* (15 Jan. 2018), https://www.theguardian.com/lifeand-
style/2018/jan/15/is-28-hours-ideal-working-week-for-healthy-life

6 David Derbyshire, 'Daytime nap "is as refreshing as a night's sleep"',
Daily Telegraph (23 June 2003), http://www.telegraph.co.uk/news/worldnews/
northamerica/usa/1433851/Daytime-nap-is-as-refreshing-as-a-nights-sleep.
html

7 'Napping', National Sleep Foundation (n.d.), https://sleepfoundation.org/
sleep-topics/napping

8 The Daily Dozers, '8 Famous Nappers in History', MattressFirm (13 Mar.
2017), https://www.mattressfirm.com/blog/current-news/8-famous-nappers-
history/

9 Hilary Brueck, '"You can sleep when you're dead" is actually deadly
advice, according to experts', Business Insider (11 Nov. 2017), http://
uk.businessinsider.com/how-much-sleep-is-enough-health-risks-
dangers-of-sleep-deprivation-2017-11?utm_source=pocket&utm_
medium=email&utm_campaign=pockethits&r=US&IR=T

10 Dan Schawbel, 'Cali Williams Yost: Why We Have to Rethink Work Life
Balance', Forbes (9 Jan. 2013), https://www.forbes.com/sites/danschaw-
bel/2013/01/08/cali-williams-yost-why-we-have-to-rethink-
work-life-balance/#6512b65331d6

11 Max Chafkin, 'Yahoo's Marissa Mayer on Selling a Company While
Trying to Turn It Around', Bloomberg Businessweek (4 Aug. 2016), https://
www.bloomberg.com/features/2016-marissa-mayer-interview-
issue/

12 Lev Grossman, 'Runner-up: Tim Cook, the Technologist', *Time* (19 Dec.
2012), http://poy.time.com/2012/12/19/runner-up-tim-cook-the-technologist/

13 Tony Poulos, 'Should untrained under-18s banned by law from social
media?', DisruptiveViews (17 Oct. 2017), https://disruptiveviews.com/
under-18s-banned-social-media/

14 Cathy Engelbert and John Hagel, 'Radically open: Tom Friedman on
jobs, learning, and the future of work', Deloitte Insights (31 July 2017), https://
dupress.deloitte.com/dup-us-en/deloitte-review/issue-21/tom-friedman-inter-
view-jobs-learning-future-of-work.html

15 Kim Janssen, 'Social media may be as bad as smoking, Kickstarter CEO
tells Ashton Kutcher'. *Chicago Times* (28 July 2016) http://www.chicagotrib-
une.com/news/chicagoinc/ct-ashton-kutcher-kickstarter-0729-chicago-inc-
20160728-story.html

16 Lynn Enright, 'Why is everything so urgent? And what's it doing to our

brains?', The Pool (17 Nov. 2017), https://www.the-pool.com/life/life-honestly/2017/46/lynn-enright-on-the-urgency-of-online-life-in-2017?utm_source=today&utm_campaign=dba5322d2c-EMAIL_CAMPAIGN_2017_10_26&utm_medium=email&utm_term=0_0522b4f78a-dba5322d2c-69280381&mc_cid=dba5322d2c&mc_eid=06d8aad68f

17 Roger McNamee, 'How Facebook and Google threaten public health – and democracy', Guardian (11 Nov. 2017), https://amp.theguardian.com/commentisfree/2017/nov/11/facebook-google-public-health-democracy

18 Patrick Nelson, 'We touch our phones 2,617 times, a day, says study', Network World (7 July 2016), https://www.networkworld.com/article/3092446/smartphones/we-touch-our-phones-2617-times-a-day-says-study.html

19 Paul Lewis, '"Our mind can be hijacked": the tech insiders who fear a smartphone dystopia', Guardian (6 Oct. 2017), https://www.theguardian.com/technology/2017/oct/05/smartphone-addiction-silicon-valley-dystopia?CMP=share_btn_tw

20 Amy B. Wang (Washington Post), 'Ex-Facebook executive says social media are destroying society', Houston Chronicle (updated 13 Dec. 2017), http://www.chron.com/business/technology/article/Ex-Facebook-executive-says-social-media-is-12425734.php

21 Martha Lane Fox, 'Technology is a marvel – now let's make it moral', Guardian (10 Apr. 2017), https://www.theguardian.com/commentisfree/2017/apr/10/ethical-technology-women-britain-internet

22 Jess Commons, 'How Did World News Drive These Women To Breaking Point?',Refinery29(16Nov.2017),http://www.refinery29.uk/world-news-anxiety-twitter-facebook

23 'Brief diversion vastly improve focus, researchers find', Science Daily (8 Feb. 2011), https://www.sciencedaily.com/releases/2011/02/110208131529.htm

Chapter 6

1 'The 2017 State of Telecommuting in the U.S. Employee Workforce', Flexjobs (n.d.), https://www.flexjobs.com/2017-State-of-Telecommuting-US/

2 https://www.thetimes.co.uk/article/ease-off-those-emails-and-smart-phones-when-youre-at-work-says-twitter-boss-w6dg6kdxg?shareToken=77567a582775fe8f51402e1b02f6257a

3 V.C. Hahn and C. Dormann, 'The role of partners and children for employees' psychological detachment from work and well-being', Journal of Applied Psychology, 98(1), 26–36, APA PsycNET, http://psycnet.apa.org/record/2012-28973-001

4 The Future of Work and Death (2016), directed by Sean Blacknell and Wayne Walsh, http://www.imdb.com/title/tt5142784/

5 SWNS, 'Half of millennials have a "side hustle"', New York Post (14 Nov. 2017), https://nypost.com/2017/11/14/half-of-millennials-have-a-side-hustle/

6 Thomas Costello, 'How to pursue your passion and launch a Side Hustle' [blog], GoDaddy (10 Apr. 2017), https://uk.godaddy.com/blog/pursue-passion-launch-side-hustle/

7 Mark Molloy, 'CEO praised for wonderful response to employee's mental health email', *Daily Telegraph* (12 July 2017), http://www.telegraph.co.uk/health-fitness/mind/ceo-praised-wonderful-response-employees-mental-health-email/

8 Helen Leggatt, 'Mobile workers sleeping with their smartphones', BizReport, (30 May 2011), www.bizreport.com/2011/05/mobile-workers-sleeping-with-their-smartphones.html

9 BBC News, 'Virgin's Richard Branson offers staff unlimited holiday' BBC (24 Sept. 2014), http://www.bbc.co.uk/news/business-29356627

10 Joe Lazauskas, 'Why More Tech Companies Are Rethinking Their Perks', *Fast Company* (16 Oct. 2015), https://www.fastcompany.com/3052329/why-more-tech-companies-are-rethinking-their-perks

11 Anne Perkins, 'Richard Branson's "unlimited holiday" sounds great – until you think about it', *Guardian* (25 Sept. 2014), https://www.theguardian.com/commentisfree/2014/sep/25/richard-branson-unlimited-holiday-job-insecurity

12 Suzanne Moore, 'It's not a perk when big employers offer egg-freezing – it's a bogus bribe', *Guardian* (26 Apr. 2017), https://www.theguardian.com/society/commentisfree/2017/apr/26/its-not-a-perk-when-big-employers-offer-egg-freezing-its-a-bogus-bribe

Chapter 7

1 Stefan Stern, 'Why have job titles become so complicated?', *Guardian* (5 Oct.2017),https://www.theguardian.com/commentisfree/2017/oct/05/job-titles-bbc-identity-architects

2 Timothy Ferriss, Tribe of Mentors (London: Vermilion, 2017)

3 Cathy Engelbert and John Hagel, 'Radically open: Tom Friedman on jobs, learning, and the future of work', Deloitte Insights (31 July 2017), https://dupress.deloitte.com/dup-us-en/deloitte-review/issue-21/tom-friedman-inter-view-jobs-learning-future-of-work.html

4 Brigid Schulte, *Overwhelmed: Work, Love, and Play When No One Has the Time*, London: Bloomsbury 2014

5 Bruce Daisley, 'The Way We're Working Isn't Working' [podcast], Eat SleepWorkRepeat(22May2017),https://www.acast.com/eatsleepworkrepeat/17-thewaywereworkingisntworking

6 Madeleine Dore, 'Why you should manage your energy, not your time', BBC(13June2017),http://www.bbc.com/capital/story/20170612-why-you-should-manage-your-energy-not-your-time

Chapter 8

1 David Goldman, 'Facebook claims it created 4.5 million jobs', CNN Tech (20 Jan. 2015), http://money.cnn.com/2015/01/20/technology/social/facebook-jobs/index.html

2 Lisa Miller, 'The Ambition Collision', The Cut (6 Sept. 2017), https://www.thecut.com/2017/09/what-happens-to-ambition-in-your-30s.html

3 Katty Kay and Claire Shipman, 'The Confidence Gap', *The Atlantic* (May 2014) https://www.theatlantic.com/magazine/archive/2014/05/the-confidence-gap/359815/

4 'Young women facing career confidence crisis, with 23% of those currently without a mentor seeking one for advice and skills development', Monster(n.d.),http://info.monster.co.uk/young-women-facing-career-confidence-crisis/article.aspx

5 https://www.equalityhumanrights.com/en/our-work/news/pregnancy-and-maternity-discrimination-forces-thousands-new-mothers-out-their-jobs

6 'How do I ask to change my working hours?', Working Families (n.d.), https://www.workingfamilies.org.uk/articles/flexible-working-after-30th-july-2014-a-guide-for-employees/?gclid=EAIaIQobChMIo_WPgYPI1wIVS7vtCh15JwWeEAAYASAAEgL_w_D_BwE

7 Kim Parker and Wendy Wang, *Modern Parenthood*, 'Chapter 1: Changing Views About Work', Pew Research Center (14 Mar. 2013), http://www.pewsocialtrends.org/2013/03/14/chapter-1-changing-views-about-work/

8 Christina Lemieux, 'Agencies need to harness the power of part-timers', Campaign(14Mar.2017),https://www.campaignlive.co.uk/article/agencies-need-harness-power-part-timers/1427177

9 Jonathan Heaf, 'How to spot: The slashie', *GQ* (15 Oct. 2017), http://www.gq-magazine.co.uk/article/how-to-spot-the-slashie

10 Plutarch, *The Parallel Lives*, (published in Vol. VII of the Loeb Classical Library edition, 1919) [online facsimile], http://penelope.uchicago.edu/Thayer/e/roman/texts/plutarch/lives/caesar*.html

11 Steve Heighton, 'Digital Distraction Is Bad for Creativity', *The Walrus* (30 Nov. 2017), https://thewalrus.ca/digital-distraction-is-bad-for-creativity/

12 Jean M. Twenge, 'Have Smartphones Destroyed a Generation?', The Atlantic (3 Aug. 2017), https://www.theatlantic.com/amp/article/534198/

13 Vivek Murthy, 'Work And The Loneliness Epidemic', *Harvard Business Review* (n.d.), https://hbr.org/cover-story/2017/09/work-and-the-loneliness-epidemic

Chapter 9

1 Caitlin Moran, 'My posthumous advice for my daughter', *The Times* (13 July 2013), https://www.thetimes.co.uk/article/my-posthumous-advice-for-my-daughter-qkjgh7whg9l

2 Lee Price, 'How to be the person people want to talk to at networking events', Monster, https://www.monster.com/career-advice/article/networking-advice-tips-0816'

3 Mercedes Cardona, 'The Future Is Automated For The People, According To Webby Trend Talk', Velocitize (26 Oct. 2017), https://velocitize.com/2017/10/26/webby-awards-wpe-summit-this-automated-life/

4 Amber van Natten, 'How Journalist Ann Friedman Built A Newsletter Empire', NewsCred (31 Mar. 2015), https://insights.newscred.com/how-journalist-ann-friedman-built-a-newsletter-empire/

Chapter 10

1 Dan Kadlec, 'Is It Rude to Talk About Money? Millennials Don't Think So', *Money* (21 Jan. 2016), http://time.com/money/4187855/millennials-money-manners/

2 Rachel Krantz, 'How To Get A Raise No Matter What, According To Businesswoman Cindy Gallop', *Bustle* (16 Dec. 2015), https://www.bustle.com/articles/129373-how-to-get-a-raise-no-matter-what-according-to-business-woman-cindy-gallop

3 Manoj Arora, '7 Income Streams of most millionaires', LinkedIn (1 Nov. 2015), https://www.linkedin.com/pulse/7-income-streams-most-millionaires-manoj-arora

4 James Pratley, 'The Side Hustle: Kodes Accessories', Starling Bank (4 Oct. 2017), https://www.starlingbank.com/blog/the-side-hustle-kodes-accessories/

5 Charlotte Cowles, 'Will I Ever Have Enough Money?', The Cut (10 Nov. 2017), https://www.thecut.com/2017/11/money-mom-will-i-ever-have-enough-money.html?utm_campaign=Ask-Polly-2017-11-15&utm_medium=email&utm_source=Sailthru&utm_term=Subscription-List-Subscription-List—Ask-Polly

6 'Josephine Cumbo, 'Saving for retirement: how much is enough?', *FinancialTimes*(16Nov.2017),https://www.ft.com/content/8e324baa-c86f-11e7-ab18-7a9fb7d6163e

7 Report, 'Bridging the Young Adults Pension Gap', YouGov (9 May 2017), https://reports.yougov.com/reportaction/pensiongap_17/Marketing

8 'Rebellious Renters', Boring Money (accessed 19 April 2018), https://www.boringmoney.co.uk/belong/rebellious-renters/

Acknowledgements

First up, I have to thank my incredible literary agent Abigail Bergstrom. Thank you for your continuous support, I'm so lucky to have you! I can't thank you enough for putting up with my many wobbly late-night WhatsApp messages. You're the best.

A huge thank you to the Hodder & Stoughton team who showed such enthusiasm for this book and the message behind it since our very first meeting (that was a good day – eating ice-cream in a boardroom on a beautiful summer's day in London). A huge thank you to my editor Briony Gowlett, you are an absolute joy to work with: seriously, thank you!!! Thanks also to Vero, Heather, Caitriona, Dom, Rosie, Cameron and Amy for being such a great team. Also, thank you to the talented Holly McGlynn for taking the photo on the back cover.

Massive thanks to Diving Bell, the coolest management team – Kim Butler, you are a BOSS. I'm so glad we met each other by accident one rainy December evening in 2016; thank goodness both of us decided to go along to that party. I didn't know at the time that I would gain such an incredible future team-mate and friend.

Thank you to all the magical multi-hyphenates included in the book: thank you for letting me interview you or letting me use your story as a case-study. I am so grateful for your contribution and time.

Thanks to anyone who has listened to or been a guest on my *Ctrl Alt Delete* podcast. So many ideas and thought-starters for the book were born out of those magical and unfiltered conversations with many different activists, creatives and entrepreneurs and I am infinitely grateful to anyone who continues to engage with the show and the subject matter. I still love making it. Thank you to Shola Aleje for brilliantly producing my live episodes.

Thank you to the amazing women at WeWork and at Bumble (Annabelle, thank you!) for collaborating with me and supporting the Multi-Hyphen movement. Thank you to my friends at Starling Bank for all that you do to push forward vital conversations around money.

Thank you to my Dad, the first self-employed multi-hyphenate I ever observed and learned from, and Mum: thank you for everything. Shout-out to my siblings, you make me feel like I'm in the coolest crew; my best friends (you know who you are aka 'The Susans'.) Paul, thanks for listening to me chew your ear off every night for a year about this book. I love our exciting, creative, multi-hyphenate life together.

Index